The Change Flywheel

Maximise energy, minimise chaos and
create momentum for meaningful change.

SAM JAYASURIYA

EARLY REVIEWS

"*The Change Flywheel* is a life-affirming read which re-connected me with my childhood, my education, my parenting, and my creativity along with so much more. It gave me cause to reflect on society and how we need to do better in terms of understanding the answer to the Masai question, "How are the children?" The recommended exercises are helpful, and I gained much inspiration which helped me reaffirm my commitment to my own learning and creativity and most importantly of all my own self-care."

Karen Smart, Head of Consultancy, AoEC

"At a time when we are rightfully reflecting on the pressures of school leadership, Samantha presents a coaching model that supports leaders to reflect on our practice. It provides guidance on making simple changes that will develop our qualities as leaders, alongside making positive improvements for our own wellbeing."

Claire Hargreaves, Deputy headteacher

"This is an excellent read, Its opening sentence is 'This book is for those who want the best for others ', and it is clear from the start that this is exactly what the author wants for her readership. The book sets out bravely to support every reader to become the best person that they can be whilst developing a greater understanding of themselves. This would be a very useful book for anyone working in education or who strives to lead, help and support others. It provides material that can be returned to again and again and will aid the growth of confidence and self-belief."

Sue Tanton, retired teacher and Education Advisor

"Finally, a book that approaches leadership with empathy. It equips leaders, both new and experienced, with techniques and insights that provide both an emphasis on self-care and practical strategies, allowing them to unlock their true potential and deliver excellent results for their organisation."

Reshma Jobanputra, business and marketing strategist, Velocity Coaching Services

"For any busy human who leads teams or helps others through their work, this is a must read. You can pick it up and choose a section that has most relevance to you at that point in your life and find inspiration and practical advice. It's prodded my brain, made me sit up and think and given me new ways to approach client challenges. As always with Sam, it's human, thought provoking and makes you see yourself through an array of lenses."

Rebecca Walker, Leadership Coach, Unfold Ltd

"This book grabbed my attention from the beginning as Jayasuriya's statement of 'serving others is an integral part of your life' chimed with my personal and professional principles. I found it refreshing to have a book about personal qualities that enliven change rather than a series of steps for organisational or cultural change. People lead change, not a process map! As a coach, mentor coach, and coaching supervisor, I am immediately reflecting on how I build momentum in my personal, professional, and practice lives to activate real change. And I'm still on the introduction."

Yvette Elcock, ICF PCC Coach, Mentor Coach, and Coaching Supervisor, Director, Moonraker Development Services Ltd

"One of my key takeaways from Sam's beautifully written book is that 'the simplest things are the best'. If indeed we cannot save time, but only use it wisely, as Sam quotes, then I take the opportunity to recommend something simple we can all do with the time we each have: read this book! It will inspire and boost your confidence to enhance the way you lead and support others, in an energising, positive and life-changing way, as it did me."

Sarah Szekir-Papasavva, Virtual Assistant, Apt Virtual Assistance Ltd

"I really enjoyed learning about *The Change Flywheel*, which I found to be a holistic and simple method of self-enquiry and self-development. The writing style is easy to read and each of the five main chapters is conveniently split into subsections that can be dipped into if time is limited. Although targeted at leaders and those working in people-helping professions, I believe it will benefit anyone who wants to develop insight and health in their relationship with themselves and others, and to create change that enables them to thrive in both their professional and personal lives."

Nicola Herbert, University Administrator

"A very clear and practical guide that every leader should read and add to their toolbox. Sam's book is full of useful exercises and activities which help create new insights and embed learning. *The Change Flywheel* model, which Sam embodies in her own life, is concise and easy to implement. It is highly effective in building resilience, a resource that is essential to navigating through these challenging times."

Carol Pearson, Executive Coach, The Pearson Practice

"Through *The Change Flywheel*, Sam provides a warm, well-researched, thought- and action-provoking read. Upon reading, you feel more self-aware, more energetically inspired, and better able to truly connect with yourself and others."

Sarah Fraser, Master Certified Coach, Happiness Express Coaching

Sam Jayasuriya © Copyright 2024

The right of Sam Jayasuriya to be identified as the author of this work has been asserted by her in accordance with the Copyright, Designs and Patents Act 1988.

All rights reserved.

No reproduction, copy or transmission of this publication may be made without express prior written permission. No paragraph of this publication may be reproduced, copied or transmitted except with express prior written permission or in accordance with the provisions of the Copyright Act 1956 (as amended). Any person who commits any unauthorised act in relation to this publication may be liable to criminal prosecution and civil claims for damage.

Although every effort has been made to ensure the accuracy of the information contained in this book, as of the date of publication, nothing herein should be construed as giving advice. Neither the author nor the publisher assumes responsibility for errors, omissions, or contrary interpretations of the subject matter herein.

The author and publisher do not accept any responsibility for any loss, which may arise as a consequence of reliance on information contained in this book.

Published by Goldcrest Books International Ltd
www.goldcrestbooks.com
publish@goldcrestbooks.com

ISBN: 978-1-911505-83-9

To my eternally beloved Carl.

You create the momentum for me to live life in harmony.

To Luc and Leo.

Light and courage always!

CONTENTS

FOREWORD	9
Introduction	11
THE CHANGE FLYWHEEL	17
CURIOSITY	23
Interview with Dara Caryotis	50
Interview with Melinda Rugani	61
COURAGE	73
Interview with Viv Grant	96
Interview with Jerome Ming	108
CREATIVITY	119
Interview with Ingrid Fetell Lee	140
Interview with Lucy Scott-Ashe	149
COMMUNITY	159
Interview with Heather Waring	179
Interview with Richard Layzell	191
CHANGE	203
Interview with me!	226
Endpiece	237
MY JOURNEY	239
Appendix	263
Acknowledgements	265
About the Author	269
References	271

FOREWORD

I first met Sam Jayasuriya several years ago when she was still working full time as a headteacher. She attended the Resilience Dynamic Accreditation Programme and has been licensed as a Community of Practice member since. So I was delighted when Sam asked me to write the foreword for her new book – *The Change Flywheel*. Sam has shared her model of operating in work and life to achieve just that and it's such a joy to witness.

As the CEO of Resilience Dynamic, I believe that in the world, resilience enables more openness, reduces stress and pressure, and brings more peace. The Resilience Dynamic community aims to make the world a better place, working as coaches to enable resilience and wellbeing in the workplace using the findings of the Resilience Dynamic research. Much of this research resonates with *The Change Flywheel*, through which Sam has empowered her clients to make a positive change in their lives and realign themselves with their values. This book is both practical and inspiring.

The Change Flywheel is a model for work and life. It's a kind of 'operating system' that will help you unlock what you really are about in this world. Written with professionals who are in the people-helping professions such as education, health/social work and others, it is a wise system for anyone.

Sam gives of herself honestly in one key chapter towards the end of the book where she describes her own personal journey and demonstrates how much her own life is influenced by *The Change Flywheel* principles. She has been a supportive and visible figure in her community encouraging others to undertake the training she outlines in her book to enhance their lives and the lives of others. If there was ever perspective to be gained through this means, this is it. There are so many words of wisdom, and several are a direct call to action!

She is a generous writer who shares her warmth, experience and wisdom. You can feel Sam's energy in every page, willing you to feel joyful and uplifted. Her energy transmits to the reader, and you can't help but feel energised to give *The Change Flywheel* a go for yourself. Who wouldn't want that same zest for life which sings throughout the book?

I have no doubt you will experience this joy also. Enjoy the read!

Jenny Campbell

> Jenny Campbell is CEO of Resilience Dynamic, set up to enable resilience for everyone. As a speaker, author of 'The Resilience Dynamic', and influencer of cultures, Jenny brings her deep multi-sectoral experience to her work, enabling organisations to see, understand and optimise the resilience of their people. She has worked with global companies and institutes, and in over 20 countries spanning five continents.

INTRODUCTION

This book is for those who want the best for others. You might be one of these people. You might be working in a people-helping profession such as HR, education, health, law enforcement or social work. There is a desire in you to work in service to others; perhaps you even see it as your life's work or calling.

You might be responsible for a team carrying out similar work to the work you used to do. The main focus of your job, however, is now on leading and managing others. This balance between leading and managing can be tough at times. Occasionally, you find yourself wishing you were back in the role you started in. It was all so much easier then.

You are having to balance that responsibility, and your ability to respond in a supportive way. Sometimes, perhaps for some of you, frequently – that can feel quite burdensome. Your personal life may be suffering or feeling squeezed.

However, serving others is an integral part of your life and work and you do it well. The downside is that you have very little time left for yourself or those close to you.

The Change Flywheel

Do any of these questions resonate with you?

- Do you feel exhausted or stressed by your work – falling asleep early, waking in the night and worrying about the work you have to do?

- Are you lacking in confidence, questioning yourself and the decisions you make? Do you feel that you are not yet at your full potential?

- Do you want to take charge of your life with a greater sense of certainty that you are on the right track?

- Are you ready for a better work/life balance, with regular routines that support you so you can also help others?

The upsides to helping others

There are many reasons to work with people. You get the opportunity to share and impart your wisdom. The work you do supports others to improve the quality of their lives as well as those they work with. Your work truly contributes to a person's mental, physical, social and spiritual health.

Perhaps you work with people because you're passionate about learning or working in a team, or because you want to give back because of the challenges you've faced in your life.

Whatever the reason, when it goes well you find yourself with a spring in your step and a sureness about the positive impact of your work on others.

The downsides to helping others

When working in a profession where the main aim is to help others, we can often forget to help ourselves. We've all heard the flight safety instructions that tell us to put our oxygen masks on before we help others with theirs. The rationale behind this is very sensible – if the cabin pressure and oxygen levels are low, there is a risk you could lose consciousness before getting the chance to assist someone else. Then what use are you?

I apply this logic to leaders and their own self-care, or lack thereof. Being a leader in a people-helping profession is no walk in the park – you face your own stresses as well as those of others. So you need to stay on top of your health in a holistic way so that you can perform and lead by example.

Many of the leaders I work with fall into the self-sacrificing pattern of serving others whilst never bringing their own physical, emotional, mental or spiritual needs to the forefront of their minds. Typically, in my experience, this leads to:

- Overwhelm – leading to stress and burnout

- Disconnect – leading to a drop in motivation and morale

- Lack of confidence – leading to a lack of agency and autonomy

Still not sure if this book is for you? Have a read of the profiles below. Please note these are not real people but common types of people I have worked with as a coach and leader. The traits they exhibit can be grouped under certain characteristics. I am going to be honest here. Some of these traits I recognise in myself and in the way I have led in the past. I have had to undo some of these traits and build new habits.

Do you recognise yourself or parts of yourself here?

Alan

If they think I'm going to change, they've got another thing coming! I've seen so many new practices over the years and they are all a rehash of the same ideas. Everything comes in cycles. If you wait around long enough, it's like buses – you will see them coming around the corner again. I have enough years of experience to see this through. If I bide my time, I can work in any new role around the roles I already have. Over time I can get it back to the way I'm familiar with. Purpose and passion – what's that? Let's leave the passion for the bedroom and the purpose for me is paying my bills.

Becki

OMG, I've got the job! How did I do that? I really didn't expect to get it. They must have only had a few people on their list. I wasn't just in the right place at the right time, there clearly was no one else around. Can I do this? I bet everyone is waiting for me to fail. I wonder if they will change their minds. Have I had an email yet to offer me the job? If I haven't heard by noon tomorrow I'll contact them myself. Or is that going to make me look like a worrier? They won't want a worrywart doing this job. Leading for me takes a lot of energy. I'm going to have to stock up on chocolate and coffee.

Introduction

Caroline People need me and rely on me. I show up every day. If I don't, who will sort out the many projects I have on my plate? My systems are perfect, if a little long-winded. If a job's worth doing, it's worth doing well. I love a good spreadsheet – it helps me keep track of the team and what's going on. If we do it my way then I know we won't miss anything. This is the most time-efficient way for me to manage my team. I have let the spreadsheet go on previous occasions but it has always ended in disaster. Oh no, I'm going to have to ring home to let them know I'll be late again.

David Oh dear, another two hours wasted on that website. If someone tracked my internet history they would laugh. Life after 50, living abroad, starting up your own business, how a dog can change your life – mmmm, maybe it was three hours, not two. It's not that I don't like my job. I just know there has to be something else. I'm only four years off early retirement – I could hang on until then. The pension people say I should work nine more years but there's no way I can wait that long. But, I also know that I don't want to just hang up my hat. They say that 50 is the new 30, but Ibiza is not what I want. In fact, in my day it was Magaluf – now I'm really showing my age! Yes, seaside life has its attractions – now where was that last tab?

Who do you identify with the most? Are you resistant to change like Alan, or fearful like Becky or are you a mix of profiles? The challenges are real and they sap the essential energy we need as people-helping professionals. I'm confident that what you read in this book will impact you in

The Change Flywheel

positive ways and help you find the momentum to make real changes in your life and your work.

This book will:

- enhance the ways you lead and support others
- provide a wealth of ideas and inspiration for those ready for a new perspective
- offer you an opportunity to self-coach
- support you to reduce overwhelm
- increase your clarity
- boost your confidence

THE CHANGE FLYWHEEL

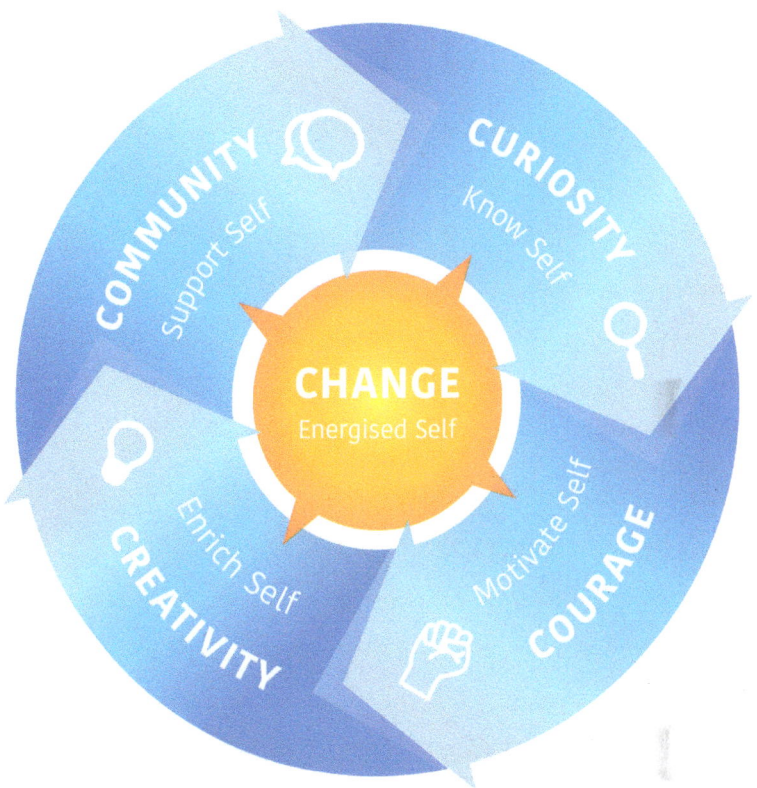

'Maximise energy, minimise chaos and create momentum for meaningful change.'

Sam Jayasuriya

The Change Flywheel

The simplest things are the best, in my opinion. An ongoing motto I use to guide me in everyday life is this: keep it simple, Sam. As people-helping professionals, we need to keep stripping back the over-complication that we tend to add to our days which takes away time and energy from our core purpose. It also dampens our excitement and enthusiasm, and this disempowers us. All of this can lead us to the three challenges that often confront people-helping professionals: overwhelm, disconnection and lack of confidence.

It was in my coach training with the Academy of Executive Coaching that my *Change Flywheel* model emerged, and I kept working on it over a few years until it found its current form.

What is a flywheel?

From a physics perspective, a flywheel is a spinning wheel, disc or rotor, rotating around its symmetry axis. As it spins it builds kinetic energy through momentum. I resonated with this idea in the work I do with both individuals and teams, so decided to bring this analogy into my coaching model.

As a Leadership Energy Coach, I know that the people I work with are often lacking in energy. What I've found is that the more self-knowledge we can gather, the more positive energy we can bring to our lives.

The Change Flywheel

The first section of my flywheel is **curiosity**. What do you need to know about yourself? The work here might be around your values, strengths and the resources you have to draw on in your work. Being curious is essential for people-helping professionals. As our focus is on others, we have to really get to know the people we support in order to not make unhelpful assumptions about what they need.

The second section is **courage**. How do you motivate yourself? How do you get out of overthinking and into action? The work here might be around building some simple habits to get you going in your work. People-helping professionals can get stuck here because they often get entrenched in seeing things from all sides, all of the time. In this ruminating space, nothing gets done and they never get off the starting blocks. There are reasons for this: people-helping professionals always want to support their team and ensure they have most if not all of their teams moving at the same time. Baby steps need to be taken to get us out of overthinking into the space of action-taking.

The third section of the flywheel is **creativity**. How do you enrich yourself? This is a key question to ask yourself as when you work with others, you tend to put the needs of others before your own. But we all know the adage, *You cannot pour from an empty cup*. Creative endeavour allows us to enter a dream-like state where future possibilities can be imagined and planned rather than only ruminated on.

The fourth section is **community** which is key to creating energy; we all know the power of that person who can sap your energy with just a look or an email. But who supports you? This is a key question that I ask my clients. Supporting voices can be found in all aspects of our lives, not just at work. For many people-helping professionals, their networks can be large but sometimes unsupportive. It's also useful to think about having some disrupters in your networks, those people who think and act in different and intriguing ways. Being clear on who supports us and what they offer us can truly enhance our networks.

The above four elements can then be woven into the **change** we want for ourselves – our future professional self who has more energy, more balance and more harmony in life. With a clearer understanding of self, my coaching clients are better equipped to explore different ways of working with others, thus creating more energy in their communities too. That kinetic energy is therefore shared with others, to everyone's benefit.

We are going to explore the five themes of *the Change Flywheel* in turn, using the same framework for each chapter. We will first explore the meaning of each word, and then look at why it is so important to us as humans and leaders. We will explore how – by developing each value within ourselves – we can foster a more rounded view of self. I will share two self-coaching activities for you to try at the end of each section and explain how each theme can support you in your role as a people-helping professional. Finally, each chapter will be

The Change Flywheel

followed by two interviews with inspiring leaders I've known, along with some further self-coaching questions.

This book is a gathering together of my learnings from a 30-year career in education and leadership. It marks a turning point in my journey as I enter my work as an elder coach and leader.

It is my wish that you gain insight into who you are and how you show up as a leader, as well as the resources to steer yourself away from overwhelm, disconnect and lack of confidence.

My *Change Flywheel* will energise you to do just that.

CURIOSITY

'Remember to look up at the stars and not down at your feet. Try to make sense of what you see and wonder about what makes a universe exist. Be curious. And however difficult life may seem, there is always something you can do and succeed at. It matters that you don't give up.'

Stephen Hawking

What is curiosity?

For as long as I can remember, my curiosity has been inspired by teachers, although not necessarily teachers in school. Teachers got me reading, told me to pull up my socks (sometimes literally) and helped push me from good to great. Teachers persevered and coached me into working through algebraic formulae, a skill I have now archived into a dusty part of my brain. Teachers reminded me that lifelong learning is a prerequisite for a life worth living, along with sustenance, sunshine, relationships and books. I took that curiosity into my life 100%.

A prime example of curiosity is the simple question:

Why?

This is a question that most of us have experienced as a child and maybe also as a parent. Studies have shown that on average a 4-year-old will ask about 300 questions a day. Busy parents are often faced with a lack of time to enter into this ping-pong of endless questions and answers with their children.

Why? can sometimes make us sigh. It's a question that can sometimes be brushed aside with comments such as 'I'll get to that later' or 'Don't ask why, just do'. How many parents reading this have answered a why with 'because I say so'? Many parents have found themselves in the terrain of toddler tantrums when tiredness – brought on by answering *why?* – has tipped into frustration.

A child's *why?* can also send us on a journey within our own minds. Why indeed can't we have ice cream for breakfast? Who makes these rules? Where did they come from?

The why? can take us on a journey of exploration along untrodden paths of parenthood we haven't considered, and down forgotten ways which can sometimes stop us in our tracks as we come across the tangled growth of unchallenged values and beliefs.

It is a question that can take us back to our own experience as children and can often reveal what our own relationship with curiosity is. Do we turn back when faced with that undergrowth or do we start to either hack or prune our way through it?

Why? is a question that some adults really do not like. And why is that?

Why? can be perceived as **judgement.**

The judgement comes from having to justify ourselves when answering simple questions like: 'Why did you do that?'

As a leader, when we are faced with why questions from employees or customers, that perceived judgement can again be found lurking beneath the surface. I have coached many leaders who have expressed abhorrence at the way they are asked a why question.

Why? can make us feel **inadequate.**

The resulting questioning in our own minds can take us to areas of knowledge which we are a little hazy about. Humans like to operate out of a place of comfort and security, so a *why?* can threaten this.

As a leader, when we feel inadequate we can sometimes get defensive; justifying the decisions we have made can make us feel in control. Constant why questions can shake what we think we have control over. A skilled leader will be able to negotiate these why questions by allowing their challenger to come up with the answer. For example: What do *you* think we should do about XYZ? What options do *you* think we have? These are questions that allow the employee to step into the problem they are seeking answers to. The tone with which a why question is asked can open or close down curiosity.

Why? can evoke **fear**.

The question can lead us to doubt our own capabilities, processes, skills or understanding of a situation. It can take us into ruminating, which can in turn bring up unsettling feelings, making us want to shut down and find safety. Adding in a question when the answer is not obvious can be scary.

Stephen Porges' work on the vagus nerve offers very relevant insights into this fear response.[1] His research shows that *'our nervous system is always trying to figure out a way for us to survive, to be safe'*.

His work on nervous system regulation can help us feel better, think better and connect better with others. So many people we work with are not functioning in a well-regulated state: either their sympathetic nervous system is working in overdrive, triggering a constant stress response, or the parasympathetic nervous system is flooding the system, leading to disconnection.

As a leader who has experienced fear when faced with traumatic experiences, I know that going into a freeze state is not what you need at these times – you need to go into action. These are the moments when the why question cannot be answered.

In my days as a deputy head, a child in my class died in the school playground at lunchtime. With no warning and despite first aid being given for a long time, the child passed away in front of the children as they played. So many people at that time asked *why?* Why didn't he live? Why did it happen then? Why did it happen to this child? The answers to these questions and more were out of my remit. I knew that this was the time to guide and protect the rest of the school. In doing that I had to consciously stop myself from going into freeze so I could support the head as we went straight into a crisis situation. What I needed to do was guide all of the children and the lunchtime staff off the playground, leaving the first aiders to do their job. I needed to be calming, reassuring, marshalling and directing. When you are in action mode, there is no time for why questions.

Why? can make us feel **guilty.**

This is another strong emotion that none of us like. Guilt can lead to defensive behaviour. Here we may find ourselves going into fight or flight mode, and gruff, blustery responses can scare the questioner away.

This guilt can lead our own inner critic to go into overdrive. Self-berating and belittling can be exhausting, once again putting us into a state of freeze.

As a leader, deflected guilt can sometimes shift into blame, such as blaming others for not doing their jobs correctly. By not acknowledging their own part in a situation, leaders can distance themselves from the ensuing chaos by not recognising the reason why something has happened. Constant blame can lead to feelings of resentment in teams. A brave leader is one who can take responsibility and even collective responsibility for issues in the organisation.

To be a great leader we need to be curious, ready to sit with the why questions for longer than a minute, and to reflect on our decisions without ruminating and jumping to answers. Good leadership is about recognising the strengths of the collective team and delegating, while letting go of the end result. A great leader uses their curiosity and their knowledge of team members to give them opportunities to come up with answers themselves; they listen and respond in a supportive way, enabling team members to grow.

Curiosity, therefore, is key for us to be able to lead our own lives, as well as to be a leader of others.

In his book 'Why, What Makes Us Curious?', astrophysicist and author Mario Livio[2] defines curiosity in these three ways:

Perceptual curiosity

This is a desire to know that is hidden deep down and triggered as soon as we are born. Striving to make sense of our place in the world, we first instinctively anchor ourselves with a caregiver for security. Within the family unit, we seek to know more and more, reaching out to grab, to test with our mouths, and always watching and listening to recognise patterns around us. This type of curiosity can be born out of striving to rectify something we don't like. It is closely linked to Livio's second definition of curiosity.

Epistemic curiosity

This is the curiosity that drives education and learning. The rewards of this curiosity can be seen in writing, artwork and scientific research. A hit of dopamine is experienced when our curiosity increases our knowledge of the world or changes others' experiences of it. That positivity can be shared with others.

Diverse curiosity

Livio also explains a different kind of curiosity which can suppress our free thinking. He calls this diverse curiosity. We see this when young people are constantly on their phones, looking for the dopamine hit given by likes and text messages from others. Our brains release dopamine irrespective of the value of the task completed.

The health warning is for all of us – not just teenagers – to watch our relationship with the digital devices that we have on us all the time. We might think we are saving time, getting our emails done, sorting out messages or escaping the boredom of daily irritations like queuing, but constantly looking down takes us away from being open and curious about the world.

A plus for our digital devices is that they do allow connection with others. Our digital communities have enabled us to increase our knowledge of the world, grow new skills and break down barriers with others. Without labouring the point, be wary that these communities do not suck you in completely. In my experience, some of the leaders I work with can often rely too much on the digital world for answers and for sharing their feelings rather than with people in their own teams. This leaves them more and more disconnected from the communities that they serve.

So now we have a sense of how important curiosity is, let's explore how we can become more curious in life.

Why does curiosity matter to us as humans?

If we think of curious people who have shaped the world we know, they are often people not bound by normal conventions; they are always questioning. The stereotypical view of curious people is those who are tenacious and investigative, traits that our education systems applaud. Curiosity can be seen in those who like space to think, to wonder and ponder life. They enjoy those quiet or empty moments that others find boring. Our education systems tend not to favour the dreamers, and the doers are the ones who have centre stage. We need to have both – time to think and time to do.

Worldwide, education systems that allow children to learn through play consistently feature highly in the PISA rankings.[3] These children have both time to do and space to think. The result is that in these countries they have more adults continuing with learning throughout their lives. They had the time to play in nature, observe living things and recognise how they fit into the world around them. They were also allowed, in that space, to be bored and think of questions they might want to ask and investigate. The Finnish curriculum has at its heart the 'joy of learning.'[4]

Curiosity and the body

A child explores the world through touch. As adults and particularly at work we can sometimes disconnect physically from our environment; we fail to sense what our inner needs are and don't think about how we navigate the world around us. In our online digital world, we are unaware of our bodies and how we sit at our desks – hunching over, straining the back, chin jutted forward to see the screen, with our feet off the ground and maybe one hooked over the back of our legs. We also forget that our bodies were made to be moved. In order to be curious, we would all benefit from taking time to pause, slow down, stop, stretch and move. The way our bodies take up space and move is called 'proprioception' and is an often underused channel.

We can enhance our curiosity by using the power of 'interoception', which is what happens within our body. This is a sense that is triggered by internal reflection. When we consciously or subconsciously trigger interoception we notice whether we are hungry or full, tired, hot or cold. This can be another underused sense that can, if not felt or responded to, trigger either emotional overwhelm or disconnection. It is the sense that my clients often find hard to tap into, forgetting to eat, pee and take a break when they are overworked. People who find it hard to focus on their bodily needs can suffer with challenges to their wellbeing. I have included a short article that talks about interoception[5] in the notes for this chapter.

We can learn to get curious about our body by following a simple mantra: pause, ponder and percolate.

- Pause, and notice what is around you

- Ponder, what physical sensations are you feeling?

- Percolate – just like a pot of coffee bubbling away, now is the time to move

We can support ourselves throughout our lives by engaging in physical exercise that enables our bodies to make sense of the world. For people-helping professionals, that might be a range of different movement types. Slower movements like yoga or pilates, tai chi, or qigong support proprioception as do faster movements like walking, running or swimming. These repetitive movements help us enter that zone of curiosity where we can better notice the world around us.

What difference does curiosity make to how I lead?

Let's link curiosity with leadership.

In thinking about the people-helping professionals I have worked with, I have created a pen portrait for a very common type of leader or person who lacks curiosity. I have called him 'Alan', in my table overleaf; you might remember him from the introduction. Here I show you how Alan's lack of curiosity can be transformed by using *The Change Flywheel* model to 'know yourself'.

Alan is leaning into that curious mindset. That feeling of trying something new and enjoying it will create new neural pathways for him. He is beginning to connect back with why he came into this particular line of work. With a curious mindset, he will discover parts of himself that he may have forgotten.

The Change Flywheel

Original complacent thought	New curious thought	Result
If they think I'm going to change they've got another thing coming!	The new changes are interesting, I am ready for new learning.	Alan is open and ready for learning. He is showing epistemic curiosity
I've seen so many new practices over the years and they are all a rehash of the same ideas. Everything comes in cycles. If you wait around long enough, it's like buses – you will see them coming around the corner again.	I can see how I might have got stuck in a rut. Some of the ways I have been working have been getting a bit stale. It's good to review working practices from time to time.	He recognises his 'stuckness' and how that has led to repetitive working practices.
I have enough years of experience to see this through. If I bide my time, I can work in any new role around the roles I already have. Over time I can get it back to the way I'm familiar with.	My experience over the past years is going to be useful and even more interesting now I have some different models to work with.	He acknowledges that he does not know everything, however long he has been in the post.
Purpose and passion – what's that? Let's leave the passion for the bedroom … the purpose for me is paying my bills.	I'm getting excited about the changes and challenges ahead. After all, they do fit in with the original reasons I came into this profession.	Alan is re-connecting with his why – why he is in the job and what it offers him.

How does a curious mindset show up for leaders?

Think about some of the most innovative companies from the last twenty years. What they have is the curiosity to expand their own knowledge not just in search of more profit, but also new and innovative ideas that will expand our reach as humans. A commendable trait of a curious person is that they are open to new thoughts from within and external to the organisation. The same applies to public sector organisations, particularly those in the education and health sector, that can often stagnate in traditional methods of procedure. I have experienced that lack of curiosity in leaders in the education sector, which in turn can lead to bored children and a curriculum that does not stimulate lifelong learning. A curious teacher can tweak a lesson and, in the process, create memories in children that can be built on in future years.

Curious leaders are often the ones who are good at seeing the world from the point of view of different stakeholders. This ability of perspective-taking is one that is consistently and constantly applied. By being able to step into the mind of the customer or client, these leaders are checking that their service or product matches the needs of their community. Being able to take different perspectives means that these leaders are dialling up their empathy skills. Being able to empathise is a core leadership skill and sits within our emotional intelligence (EI). Daniel Goleman's work on EI from the 1990s is held in high regard by people in the coaching and training industries, and beyond. His five EI competencies[6] consist of self-awareness, self-regulation, social skills, motivation and empathy. In relation to curiosity, empathy leads to questions which foster a non-judgmental approach towards our teammates and clients.

Curious people are not put off by ambiguity. They are willing to test things out, knowing that the time they take to test will pay off for all in the long term.

Curiosity in leaders leads to innovation. In our complicated world where the future can appear rather bleak – in terms of climate change and entrenched views – being curious as a leader paves the way towards a better world. What better question to ask ourselves than this:

What if more of us led from this place of curiosity?

CHANGE FLYWHEEL TAKEAWAYS

CURIOSITY – know yourself

- What makes you avoid the why questions: fear, judgement, guilt or inadequacy?

- How can you create a healthier relationship with your digital devices?

- Look at your calendar and ask yourself – where can I put in time to pause, ponder and percolate?

- Curious people are not put off by ambiguity. What is your relationship with ambiguity?

How can developing curiosity help me create my future self?

In order to truly know ourselves, we need to ask *why?* in a variety of ways.

When I started my coach training, we had to ask ourselves the question: who am I? From that one question, many why questions started to emerge. This exercise was inspired by my learning with the AoEC, a leading coaching organisation.

Activity 1: Who am I?

Time needed: Half an hour on day 1, half an hour on day 2

Aim: to find out more about who you are.

Stage 1 – first day

Find a quiet space and time in your week to do this reflection.

Prepare your mind for this work by doing some coherent breathing.[7] This is a very simple breathing technique which allows your brain to get ready to be calm and alert. The purpose is to increase your heart rate variability and balance your autonomic nervous system. The article I have linked to here gives a great explanation of why this is so helpful.

Sit or lie quietly, breathe in for 6 and out for 6. Don't hold your breath on the way in or out. Breathe through your mouth and deep into your diaphragm. As you do, imagine your breath is going in and out of your heart rather than your lungs. It might be helpful to place your hand over your heart. As you regulate your breathing, think of someone or something that gives you great joy. Let that feeling of joy wash over you. After a minute or two, get ready to ask yourself this question:

Who am I?

Now write down as many as you can of the thoughts that come into your head. Spend about a minute doing this. If it helps, imagine yourself talking to someone in a room, someone you have never met before.

It might help to start each phrase with 'I'.

If you don't like to write, you can record your voice by speaking directly into your phone. An app like Otter.ai is useful for this.

....
....
....
....
....
....
....
....
....
....
....
....
....
....
....
....
....
....
....

Stop, pause and breathe again.

Now have a look at what you have written.

Stage 2

Cover your answers, close your journal or pause the recording on your phone.

Prepare yourself again with one minute of breathing.

Now ask yourself that question again:

Who am I?

Write down as many answers as possible that you haven't already used that come to mind. Dig deep.

....
....
....
....
....
....
....
....
....
....
....
....
....
....
....

Stop, pause and breathe again.

Now have a look at what you have written. Check and make sure it makes sense.

Do not cross out anything you have written.

Stage 3

Repeat the process one more time, as per stage 2.

Who am I?

....
....
....
....
....
....
....
....
....
....
....
....
....
....
....

Stop, pause and breathe again.

Stage 4

Look at what you have written.

This is where I want you to get creative.

Using different colours or post-it notes, try to arrange the words and phrases into groups.

You might find that the first set contains a lot of labels which may have been given to you by others: *Sister, father, daughter, son, etc.*

The Change Flywheel

The second set may have more of your unique skills or strengths:

I am tidy. I am organised. I am great with complicated projects.

The third set, perhaps the smallest, may contain phrases which you have had to dig deep to find:

I am determined. I am brave.

These statements may have led you to another question:

How do I know?

Take a break here. Go off and do something else. This question needs to sit in your unconscious thinking. More ideas will float up and into your brain at different times of the day. Keep your journal or paper close by and try to capture them before they drift away.

Avoid crossing out anything on your list. This is a piece of data collection all about you.

....
....
....
....
....
....
....
....
....
....
....
....
....
....

Stage 5 – second day

Take the lists of words and phrases again that you have already started to arrange into groups.

Group them again, this time into three groups:

I am this

In this group, you might put phrases like 'I am a brother' or 'I am a driver'. Any phrase that you are happy with and that is unlikely to change, even with death.

....
....
....
....
....
....
....
....
....
....
....
....
....
....
....
....
....
....
....
....
....
....

The Change Flywheel

I want to evolve this

Here, put phrases that you know are true but also know you can develop or elevate:

'I can focus in team meetings but not on my own', 'I can swim in shallow water' or 'I can drive on quiet roads but not on dual carriageways'.

Curiosity

I want to discard this

In this final box, put the labels that you want to discard, those that have been hanging around your neck since childhood. These labels were often given to us by others and may no longer be true for you. Now, with maturity, you can let them go.

....
....
....
....
....
....
....
....
....
....
....
....
....
....
....
....
....
....
....
....

The question now is:

Who might I be?

Spend some time journaling about what you want to change. Make sure you focus first on the positive impact this change will have for you in the long term. You might be feeling a little excited. If you are feeling overwhelmed, remember they are just ideas and within every idea is a nugget of joy that will support your overwhelm, disconnection or lack of confidence.

Put a timeline in. Is this something that can be achieved in a week, month or year or might it even take years? By putting in a timeline, you are committing yourself to even thinking about taking action.

Who might I be?

……………………………………………………………………………………
……………………………………………………………………………………
……………………………………………………………………………………
……………………………………………………………………………………
……………………………………………………………………………………
……………………………………………………………………………………
……………………………………………………………………………………
……………………………………………………………………………………
……………………………………………………………………………………
……………………………………………………………………………………
……………………………………………………………………………………
……………………………………………………………………………………
……………………………………………………………………………………
……………………………………………………………………………………
……………………………………………………………………………………
……………………………………………………………………………………
……………………………………………………………………………………
……………………………………………………………………………………
……………………………………………………………………………………
……………………………………………………………………………………
……………………………………………………………………………………
……………………………………………………………………………………

Curiosity

If you have time for a bonus activity, you might enjoy a short video from psychotherapist Mel Schwarz, entitled 'Who am I?' You will find the link in the chapter references at the back of the book.[8]

So, let's go back now to that wonderful question: Why? The one we used to ask all the time as children. The one that we often forget to ask ourselves as adults.

A leader can learn so much if they are able to adopt the playful, curious mind of a child when faced with problems in their organisation.

That playful mind can be seen in the way that Sakichi Toyoda, the founder of Toyota Industries, developed the 5 Why technique[9] which was taken on and developed further by Taiichi Ohno to support Toyota in their product development in the 1950s.

His technique has been adopted by leaders across the world to help them uncover ways to develop their organisations, and it can also be used to develop yourself. The method has been adapted into various iterations, but for the purposes of this activity, I want to return to its simplest format. I am inviting you to use the 5 Whys to find out more about yourself.

Activity 2: Investigate the why

Time needed: 1 hour

Aim: to get closer to the root of a problem.

Think of a recurring thought or problem which has arisen in your life or work.

Write down the problem on one post-it note.

Then ask the first *why?* Alongside that, write the point that comes to mind.

Continue in this format until you have asked the question *why?* five times. Then look at your final *why*, the root cause, and work your first step to address it.

You might notice that the order of reasons is out of sequence.

Take a moment to reorder them.

Here is an example of how the exercise might unfold:

I'm noticing a sense of dissatisfaction with my work.

Why?

Because I have done this too many times – there is no challenge.

Why?

Because I haven't pushed myself to take on new roles and now I'm stuck.

Why?

Because I haven't consolidated my networks.

Why?

Because the organisation is taking up too much of my time.

Why?

Because I haven't developed my team enough.

First Step:

Embody curiosity; walk and talk with your team members to start to find out what they need.

Curiosity

You can write your answers in the correct order below, if you wish, or stick your post-it notes in the space.

INTERVIEW WITH DARA CARYOTIS

Dara is a woman who loves to learn about how the mind and body work together. As a coach and trainer, she works with professionals who are very busy juggling family, work and huge amounts of responsibility. She uses her lifelong learning in embodiment to support her clients to really find out who they are and to meet their potential.

Introduction

I was introduced to Dara by a fellow coach who spotted our mutual love of working with the body. As soon as I met her, I knew that she was a woman I dearly wanted to be connected to. Her warmth, enquiring personality and wide experience meant that, over time, I came to see her as a lifelong mentor and a guide in all things somatic.

Dara started her professional career as a computer scientist. It was a good way for her to earn a living and pay her bills. Alongside her computer programming knowledge, Dara was and is still passionate about embodiment. Her earliest learnings about embodiment came from her practice of Aikido, followed by yoga and shiatsu. She knew intuitively that there was intelligence in the body. Her passion for embodiment continued with a year-long course in oriental diagnosis that had to stop as her computer programming work picked up and she started to travel around the world. As parenthood beckoned, the travelling stopped and her children soon took up more of her time. As they grew older, the learning picked up again and she took a course in anatomy and physiology to add to her knowledge.

As she moved into the world of coaching, she took her passion for embodiment with her. When Marvin Oka presented at an NLP conference in 2014 she found his work inspiring. Marvin Okra and Grant Soosalu were the creators of mBIT;[10] their work translated into words what she knew from her own life. In her words, it *'totally resonated with me'*. She went on to do their training and became a course trainer herself.

I was fortunate to be introduced to Dara in 2018. As soon as we met, I knew that our paths would cross again. She and I shared a love of the natural world and as she lived nearby, we used to enjoy walks together in our local area. She had a beautiful way of inviting more embodiment into our walks, something I particularly appreciated. Dara became my mBIT trainer and guide in all things to do with embodiment. I am forever in her debt for helping me reconnect parts of me that I knew instinctively had been sidelined.

Five questions about your work and approach to life

Curiosity

In the words of Stephen Hawking: *'Remember to look up at the stars and not down at your feet. Try to make sense of what you see and wonder about what makes the universe exist.* ***Be curious.*** *And however difficult life may seem, there is always something you can do and succeed at.'*

How do you keep your curiosity alive in the work that you do today?

'I think it's innate in me to be curious. I do feel like I'm a bird looking at things from every angle. I think I need that curiosity to see every perspective.'

Dara talked about her natural curiosity and how it would show up in her work in IT and later as a consultant. Her job was basically asking a lot of questions. Now with her mBIT training, she understands that she needs the wisdom of many perspectives and particularly the three of the head, heart and gut. With her coaching clients, she is naturally curious about how she can support them. In recent months she has worked with people who identify as neurodiverse. The question she asks is this: what are the implications for their work and their personal life? She strives to be always seeking out new pieces of learning as well as keeping a sharp eye on new audiences. All in all, this helps keep her curiosity alive. She also talked about the work of Gregory Batesman[11] who wrote the book 'Ecology of the Mind'. Dara believes that his work inspired many of the NLP gurus in the late sixties and early seventies.

Dara talked about her love for being curious and, even more so, to be compassionately curious.[12] What she loves is to work with people in order to help them improve the quality of their lives. It is her passion that drives her curiosity. In establishing herself in this state, she is solely focused on positive outcomes for her clients.

Courage

It takes courage to be a leader. Thinking about the key leaders in your life, how did their courage support you to be more courageous in your life?

Dara's father was the first leader that came to her mind. One of six children, he experienced the death of his own father at the very young age of three which forced him to mature quickly and take on an adult role while still a child. From a young age, he and his brother supported the rest of his family and he ended up leaving school after a very bad experience and with little education. However, he was fortunate to have an uncle who left him some land and a house after his death and Dara's father became a farmer. Overcoming all of his early childhood challenges, he went on to have his own farm and raised ten children, including Dara. By the time of his death, the farm had grown to be very successful.

This positive role modelling showed Dara as a young adult that she could do what she wanted with hard work and persistence. She took her father's experiences into her own heart, moving away from her beloved Ireland at a young age to live in London. She never questioned whether or not she could do this as her own strong parenting figures enabled her to banish self-doubt. Now, she assumes she can do something when she puts her mind to it.

Most of her siblings have that entrepreneurial spirit, deciding what they wanted and putting in a plan to make it happen. Dara described the work of one of her sisters, Lainey, who changed her career as a lab technician, took a leave of absence and then reinvented herself as Lainey Keogh[13] – a very successful cashmere knitwear designer. One of her other sisters who moved to Australia has also been a positive role model, setting up a new life and career in sustainability.

Dara went on to describe how her father was also able to take risks, leaving the family home for a full year to work in Australia and then returning to set up a market garden, growing salad and flowers. The courage to do different things and pivot to change tack, explore the export market and be successful. Her family's business created an ideal environment for her (and her siblings) to embed the routine of diligent hard work. After school and college, Dara and her siblings all did time out on the farm; Dara was convinced that her parents had had ten children precisely to have a biddable and ready workforce on hand!

A key character strength that Dara's father helped her develop is honesty.

In her professional career, Gary Boyce – her MD in the IT company – showed her the power of integrity: not letting others down and also not allowing someone else's behaviour to sway you. To Dara as a young professional, his calm and regulated manner modelled how to keep your head in challenging situations.

Dara went on to talk about how her position in the family made her a natural leveller. Given she was born after her father returned from Australia, there was a three-year gap between her and her siblings. As an adult, she always seeks the opinion of others around her and sees herself as someone who likes to include/embrace all perspectives. She views her inclusive perspective and foresight as a strength: *'I am the one who has the ability to do this, others don't.'*

A second colleague called Simon was another courageous role model. He always looked out for her and supported her in her work. One leadership quality he demonstrated was humility, showing her how to not be too egotistical about her work.

Three men and two women showed her courage: forward-thinking people who didn't just take risks but also supported their risks with hard work. Farming is risky work; you never know what is going to come up in terms of weather and disease, etc. This image of risk is not one that I would naturally assign to farming as the idea I've had is that farmers are dependable and not risk-takers. However, a farmer only has their land and in order to succeed they need courage and hard work.

Creativity

In the words of the late great Sir Ken Robinson:[14] *'I believe this passionately that we don't grow into creativity; we grow out of it or rather we get educated out of it.'*

What advice would you give schools to help children develop their creative thinking?

'I would go into the body again.'

When Dara learnt NLP she thought that every teacher should do a 4-day course in it. NLP is all about language, communication and beliefs. Every single child needs to understand the power of language and the choices that they make with their words.

The destructive work of teachers who do not use language correctly can destroy children's beliefs about themselves, causing blocks that can take years to dismantle.

Dara is a massive proponent of movement – anything that allows children to be outdoors or with music regularly. Children need to recognise how their bodies feel different when they move them in different ways and learn to use words to express and understand the differences they feel. In her opinion, the current UK curriculum is far too narrow in this respect.

In bringing about creative change, Dara would always start with the teacher before she would start with the school. And I agree with her that there needs to be a fundamental change in teacher training so that all teachers know about *'somatic intelligence and about the power of language.'* Humans are built for connection and for living in tribes together, something which is particularly needed in the world we live in where technology can often separate us.

Her adage would be this: to keep it simple. The simplest thing is to allow children to *'walk out a story'*, just as she does when she's working on a speech or some new training. How would that work for children? A trusted adult would walk with a child who is allowed to share what was on their mind regarding an incident or issue. By walking, talking and stopping from time to time, the child can start to embody their part in the story and any actions that they might need to take.

Community

For many years, I have had a postcard above my desk outlining '44 ways to build community'. What communities do you lead or have you led in the past, and what helped them grow?

'My part in the family is to keep the family gelling.'

The community Dara was talking about here was her family; she is the person who gets called when there are problems in the family. She replenishes them and they are very important to her.

Expanding to her circle of friends, she played the part of bringing people together. She would state her intention for a gathering and invite friends to join. She led by action and her friends and colleagues would join. Dara still loves these mini-communities that come together with a clear purpose in mind.

Moving to her mBIT community, Dara was at the forefront of the spread of this work, making and keeping good firm connections with thought leaders who were working with the body. As one of the early trainers in mBIT, Dara was immersed in a world that was burgeoning with new ideas. It was around the same time that *HeartMath* came into being. Although the mind-body connection was not a new idea, it wasn't as known in the Western world as it is right now. Being at the forefront of new ideas isn't actually what drives Dara – it is communities coming together to discover and explore new ideas. She loves bringing people together to share ideas, be creative and have experiences. Dara loves to co-create with others. She has learnt to use the multi-faceted intelligence in her body and that she can create something much better when she has input from others:

'The outcome that one person will create generally is not as good as an outcome that two or three people will create. So create together.'

Dara has both generosity and perseverance – a commitment to working with a team and seeing things through. That's what keeps her communities thriving.

Change

Change is the only constant in our lives or so the saying goes. How do you navigate change while keeping harmony in your life and work?

Although there was consistency throughout much of Dara's young life on the farm – the sowing, the planting and the harvesting – there was always change. The seasons changed, as did the weather; each day was different. People in the house were different each day and no day was exactly the same. This acceptance of life as it is was taken into her work with her clients. Her job now is to listen and question but not to use the same recipe for each client. Just as the farm was created together as a family, Dara co-creates with her clients.

What helps her keep that acceptance and harmony in her life is her daily meditation practice. She meditates for 21 minutes every day, practising heart-focused breathing. She consciously connects with appreciation, gratitude and compassion. Every Monday morning she gathers together with a larger group and again meditates for 21 minutes. Meditation is what gives her inner strength and this resourcefulness has been a support to her family. She is fully committed to this daily practice because it helps her deal with anything.

You might be wondering – why 21 minutes? Dara loves multiples of three. She also knew that she needed the consistency of a daily habit to make it a lifelong one. She had a tendency to breathe very shallowly and knew that it would take daily practice to learn to breathe deeply and naturally by default.

How does Dara embody my *Change Flywheel* coaching model?

Dara's birdlike curiosity gives her the opportunity to view life from all perspectives, from the close-up to the far-away. This skill allows her learning to evolve in a very natural way. The courage of her immediate family to strike out and use the land to support their lives is seen in the way that Dara motivates herself, keeping the body central to all the work she does. Her creativity in linking aspects of her work life to support the communities around her makes her a truly supportive and encouraging person to be around. Her daily habits bring her harmony and one feels a sense of peace in her presence.

DARA'S TAKEAWAYS

Curiosity: Take a bird's eye view of a current problem, from up above in the clouds to down on the ground. What else do you see?

Courage: What would be the biggest risk you could take now? List out the pros and the cons.

Creativity: Moving our bodies is the best way to get to know them. What 10-minute movement could you add into your day?

Community: When was the last time you used more than one brain to create something new? What was the outcome and how might it have been different if you had only used one?

Change: Coherent breathing of 6 counts in and 6 counts out works. Test this out for 2 minutes for a week and see what a difference it can make to your life.

INTERVIEW WITH MELINDA RUGANI

Melinda is a designer, collector and all-round creator. She is the mistress of reinvention but there is a thread of curiosity holding all of her work together. Her last project was designing and making hand-embroidered bags which are all linked by a theme. Each bag is focused on a key creative leader from history, featuring vintage lace and beads, with a unique story stitched in.

Introduction

As my oldest sister, Melinda Rugani has inevitably had a big impact on my life. Not only did she care for me on many occasions when our mum was working, but she also inspired the development of my own mindset through her creative endeavours.

As the youngest in our family of five with a mother who worked constantly, I always looked to my siblings for guidance. Melinda provided a lot of inspiration and still does to this day. The creator gene is very strong in her and her appreciation for beauty in the world is mirrored in her work. I also see great courage in Melinda, choosing to make her home in another part of the world. Perhaps it's the role of an older sibling to strike out and be adventurous. Who knows? I am grateful to have her in my life and look forward to seeing what she gets up to next.

Five questions about your work and approach to life

Curiosity

In the words of Stephen Hawking: *"Remember to look up at the stars and not down at your feet. Try to make sense of what you see and wonder about what makes the universe exist. Be **curious**. And however difficult life may seem, there is always something you can do and succeed at.'*

How do you keep your curiosity alive in the work that you do today?

'*I talk to people. I love finding out about them and their interests.*'

Melinda related this back to a time in her teens in the late sixties, when she realised her curiosity was a useful resource in her life:

'*As a 16-year-old teenager of colour, who didn't have a boyfriend, I sat and thought ... How can I talk to boys?*'

The result of her reflections was a decision to be interested in what the young men at that time were interested in. Finding out about the offside rule in football, for example, added to her ability to communicate with a wider variety of people. As a result, she had no problem finding a partner and new friends who welcomed a curious mind.

Melinda's curiosity also supported her in work that was not quite as creative as she would have liked. For example, in her early thirties, she found herself working in the BBC's finance department. Although she disliked maths, she found that she was good at certain aspects of it, for example – data finance: 'I had the tenacity to look for something. I could be their problem-solver.'

Melinda had found persistence and perseverance in her curiosity. She also related how that curiosity had led to moments of happiness in her work:

'Being curious leads to joy.'

That same joy was felt in her everyday life. As a young child, she had gone to school in Greenwich, which helped develop her curiosity in nature. As the eldest, she often took her younger siblings, including me, into the park to provide respite and quiet working time for my mother.

'Having Greenwich Park next to me captured my interest, in fact, my first fossil was found next to the statue of General James Wolf which is found high above the Thames.'

The fossil was a seashell piquing her curiosity and took her into a discussion with a teacher about how a seashell could be found inland.

That love of nature still catches her interest now but doesn't necessarily connect to her work. It has continued to feature in her personal life, including tending plants and hunting fossils. She still adds to her fossil collection to this day, with a huge collection that she has a great deal of knowledge about.

Melinda also shared how her curiosity makes her a self-professed observer of people. This is something that came from her background in fashion design. As a student, she was taught to perceive the human body in specific and creative ways:

'How they moved, how they walked, sat, bent over ... because ultimately you have to take a piece of fabric to fit a 3-dimensional body which is moving.'

She was taught by her tutors to look at buildings, not straight on but from all different angles. This way of observing has been replicated many times in her life, playing out in her love of home interiors and decoration.

Out of all of the words on my *Change Flywheel*, curiosity is extremely important to Melinda. She says that it is the starting point for everything in her life.

Courage

It takes courage to be a leader. Thinking about the key leaders in your life, how did their courage support you to be courageous in your life?

At first, Melinda was unsure of whom to choose. Following on from her previous answer, she talked of *'absorbing'* a bit of everything and everyone.

'There are a myriad of people from different walks of life. You take a bit of all of them.'

But then she talked about our mother. She recognised Mum's courage and relayed particular memories which stood out for her.

As a young child, she became aware of some sadness in Mum ... the sadness of being so disconnected from her homeland and family. These memories were tied to the joy that Mum shared with her when she received a letter from her own mother.

Interview with Melinda Rugani

Our mother had come from a home with servants in Sri Lanka. She did not know how to cook. Arriving in London in the late fifties, she had to deal with all of the new responsibilities that were thrown at her. The winter of 1960 was a tough one but even through that, Mum had to care for her two young children.

Snow was a treasured memory for Melinda; she remembered our mother being outside in her sari collecting snow in a little sandcastle bucket just so she could feel the magic of this unfamiliar weather.

Our father wasn't around much as he was working, and Mum was the one who had to cope with the racial slurs along with her two small children. Life in the sixties was tough but my sister's memories of Mum were of a very courageous woman.

This courage supported Melinda to see the world through the eyes of someone bravely overcoming adversity.

'It was the platform that you bounce off ... you don't consciously think of these things. You gather in all the other people that you have admired through the periods of development times and you bring those on board as well.'

Growing up in an immigrant family, with our mother trying to protect us from the challenges of that, meant Melinda felt quite isolated as a teenager. She felt that she was a bit of an outsider and, like many youngsters of that era, lived her life through music and TV.

Melinda also drew courage from the Apollo astronauts, whom she followed with great enthusiasm around the time of the lunar landings in the late sixties and early seventies. She filled scrapbooks with cuttings and photos of them from newspapers and magazines. Their courageous endeavours inspired her view that life was out there, somewhere else in the universe, and maybe that life had visited Earth sometime in the past.

Creativity

In the words of the late great Sir Ken Robinson: *'I believe this passionately that we don't grow into creativity; we grow out of it or rather we get educated out of it.'*

What advice would you give schools to help children develop their creative thinking?

'Honestly, I believe that children need to have a lot of free time. When we were children, we had a lot of free time and limited resources.'

With these limited resources, Melinda made many things. She learnt to occupy herself with paper, cereal boxes and packing crates to satisfy that curiosity of hers. She even remembered a time when she used my old pram to make a go-cart. Helped by our father, she used the wheels for the chassis and wood from a crate.

The joy of creating in those spare moments took her outside a lot – moments which, these days, would probably be taken up by screen time. This spare time allowed her to really develop her creations. Inspired by the many cowboy films of the time, she once spent hours working on making the perfect bows and arrows.

Time to create in her childhood gave her the process that she still uses up to this day:

'When I want to make something, in my head I have to imagine the whole process from start to finish. I need to have that information in my head in order to draw something on a piece of paper.'

She recognises that as an introvert who shows up in the world as an extrovert, she enjoys that time in her head:

'Time to fail, play, time to think it out.'

Melinda talked about how children also need to be told stories and be able to interact between reality and fantasy. She saw this as a fundamental way to support creativity. By hearing stories, children can then make up their own stories.

Melinda is, essentially, a creator. Currently, she is sewing and designing using vintage fabrics. She also works as a support in her local school on Bonny Doon Mountain in Santa Cruz. Surrounded by Redwoods and ancient Scots pines, she gives the children space and time to think:

'You can't be creative in a dark room. You can't be creative if it is always structured. You can't be creative if that structure is too rigid.'

Schools also need to give children time to be quiet within themselves. Just as I always say as part of my coaching support, we all need time to think, rather than always being busy busy busy…

Community

For many years, I have had a postcard above my desk outlining '44 ways to build community'. What communities do you lead or have you led in the past, and what helped them grow?

Melinda is passionate about community:

'Community is and always will be your support when you really need it. But communities need your investment.'

She is also a keen community builder.

'You don't need to be a mayor of a town, but you need to know your neighbours. I don't need to be in their pocket or vice versa but I need to know who they are, knowing what they can offer.'

Her artistic community, where she currently lives, offers her a lot. This includes practical support, important when living somewhere relatively remote, as well as creative support when she is working on a new idea.

Melinda lived for many years in the arty community of Whitstable, in Kent, and was one of the founding members of a local arts group. Collaborating with others, she initiated work on building an arts centre which started life as a barge on the beach. She recognised that coming together with others and making a strategic plan was what got stuff done.

Her curiosity and creativity also supported a pop-up gallery sited in the old Fishmongers on Whitstable High Street. By mucking in to help a girl paint the shop, she was then able to showcase her own handmade shell jewellery there. She saw how using disused properties in this way brought life to the town. This was all before Whitstable Contemporary Arts came into being.

Now, as part of the Bonny Doon community in Santa Cruz, Melinda has supported many groups. Although she is not religious, she has supported church coffee mornings, and also joined the ladies' group and helped the fire service with fundraising breakfasts and dinners. By supporting others, she found she was also supported during a challenging period when battling breast cancer. More recently the community rallied to support her and her husband, with dinners being cooked and a beautiful patchwork quilt hand-sewn to bring her comfort. This community continues to support her as she continues her challenges with cancer.

Melinda firmly believes that we all can do something in our community. Her suggestion is to get involved in a local charity sale, take a dog for a walk or volunteer in a local school. These small acts of kindness are what make a community strong.

Change

Change is the only constant in our lives **or so the saying goes. How do you keep harmony in your life or in your work?**

'Change and curiosity go hand in hand. So if you are curious about something, things will change. It has to be a given ... your brain will adapt and follow a path and create that change.'

Melinda believes that for harmony to override stress, you need to draw on curiosity. If you are stressed, you need to pause, get curious and try a different path. In doing so, we can help alleviate other people's stress too while creating more harmony in our own lives.

'Our curiosity will bring you courage, creativity, community and change.'

As a final thought, Melinda added:

'In my life, I live in the present and possibly into next week.'

The Change Flywheel

How does Melinda embody my *Change Flywheel* coaching model?

Melinda's curiosity is always sparked by her observations of life and people. Following through with her observations, she has also shown that she is skilled at creating new communities around her. Her creative endeavours really feed her soul, generating impetus for more growth and learning. Her desire to really live in the present, particularly in recent years, has meant that she puts aside time to focus on completing projects, something which gives her great satisfaction. Her courage in meeting new health concerns head-on shows a resolve and determination that many would be hard-pressed to find.

MELINDA'S TAKEAWAYS

Curiosity: *'You have to observe people.'* Who do you know in your team? Do you really know them? What else can you find out about them from observing?

Courage: Remind yourself of a time in your life when you had to prove your worth, against the odds. What helped you overcome that challenge from others?

Creativity: *'Time to fail, play, time to think it out.'* When was the last time you failed at a project? How can you get more comfortable with failing?

Community: *'Community needs your investment.'* Which of the communities in your life need a bit more 'money in the bank', so to speak? Whether that's time, energy or other resources, what would that investment give you in your life?

Change: *'In my life, I live in the present and possibly into next week.'* Past, future or present – what takes up most of your thoughts?

COURAGE

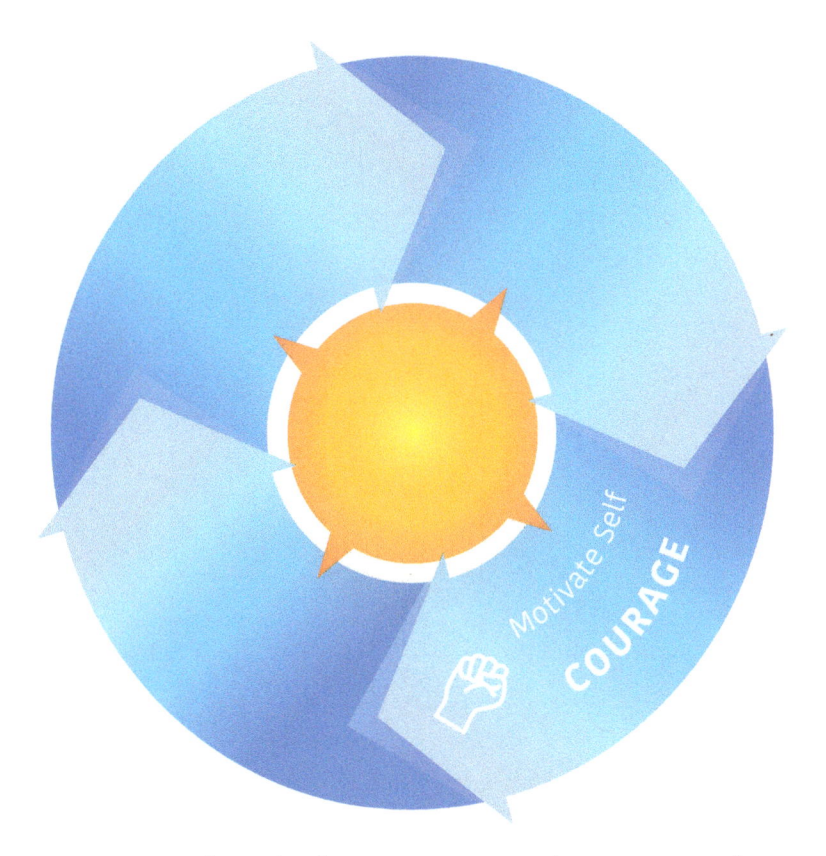

'Courage doesn't always roar, sometimes courage is the little voice at the end of the day that says I'll try again tomorrow.'

Mary Anne Radmacher

What is courage?

As Dorothy, Toto, the Tin Man and the Scarecrow walked through the Land of Oz they entered a dark and gloomy forest. Watching that scene from The Wizard of Oz at eight years old, I felt scared – scared because of the fairy tales I had been told of wolves and other dangers lurking in dark places. My lack of courage was felt in a physical and emotional sense. I pressed my back into the chair, holding myself on the seat, willing the characters to go another way.

Throughout the film, courage is explored in many different ways.

The scarecrow recognises that he does have **intellectual courage**. He shows all the way through that he wants to learn and can apply that learning to the journey with his companions.

The Tin Man realises that he does have the **emotional courage** that he seeks and opens his heart to accept and give love to the world.

The Lion initially displays his **physical courage** when first encountering Dorothy and her companions but is not able to follow through, instead expressing his woe with big tears as Dorothy smacks him on the nose. He is later redeemed by standing firm and facing the witch's army.

Dorothy shows **social courage** in standing up to the Wicked Witch of the West throughout her journey. She never turns back but pushes on, supporting the others on the way and finally throwing the fatal bucket of water over the witch's head.

As the Wizard is unmasked, he has the **moral courage** to do what he knows to be right – to get Dorothy home to her family.

Finally, **spiritual courage** is shown by all of the characters as they recognise their place in the world, whether that be in Oz or Kansas. The story ends when they know how to live their life with purpose and meaning.

The dictionary definition of courage is:

'Being able to do something that frightens us or having the strength in the face of pain or grief.'

As I hope you have seen, courage can be much more nuanced.

I learnt about these six levels of courage from the writings of Jennifer Armstrong and Lisa Dungate.[15] Their work expands the definition above to help support children and parents. What drew me to their writing was the beautiful way they intertwined fairy stories with practical ways to live fearlessly.

We would be wise to take the learnings from each of these courage types as we move through our lives.

Intellectual courage allows us to ask questions, take time to think, wrestle with a problem and sometimes say aloud – I don't know – and then find out.

Emotional courage allows us to feel all our emotions and not put them into a hierarchical table. By allowing time to notice all emotions we can grant them equal value and equal time, and thus not allow our negative emotions to overwhelm us.

Physical courage allows us to move fearlessly in the world, sure of the limits of our own bodies. In practice, it is about taking action.

Social courage allows us to show who we are and be happy with sharing all aspects of ourselves with trusted friends and colleagues. It is all about both leading and knowing when to follow.

Moral courage allows us to rise above ridicule and do the right thing, particularly when we know deep in our hearts that action is needed.

Spiritual courage allows us to search for purpose and meaning in our lives, a core aspect of building resilience.

Why does it matter to us as humans to live courageously?

I believe that courage is key to helping us flourish. But unless we delve deeper into where courage sits in our body, our lack of courage can hold us back in all we endeavour to do in our lives.

When we see and feel courage inside we are more open to growth and moving forwards with our work and life. We inhabit a growth mindset as described by Carol Dweck PhD, one of the world's leading researchers in the field of human motivation, personality and development. Her research was published in her book, 'Mindset: The New Psychology of Success', in 2006.[16]

Her theory is that mindset is a self-perception that people hold about themselves. Fixed mindset refers to a belief that intelligence and abilities are relatively innate, changing very little over time. People with a fixed mindset will talk about their abilities and talents and not spend time growing them. In my mind what holds them back is fear. Fear enjoys eating courage for breakfast.

Fear can hold us back in many ways, including the common condition of imposter syndrome. Imposter syndrome is a collection of feelings of inadequacy that persists despite evidence of success. It is the feeling that we might be found out to be a fraud.

Studies show that 70% of people suffer from imposter syndrome at some time in their lives, with women feeling it more than men. In a recent study of female executives in the US, 75% of women surveyed were affected by imposter syndrome, with women of colour being disproportionately affected.

The term was first identified in an article written by Pauline Clance and Suzanne Imes in the late 1970s.[17] They had surveyed 162 high-achieving women who had identified with feelings of being an imposter.

Dr Valerie Young,[18] now an internationally recognised expert on Imposter syndrome, identified very strongly with these feelings as a student in the 1980s, as did many of her cohort. Along with several of her student body, she set up a support group for fellow 'imposters' to share their experiences of how this particular way of being was showing up in their lives.

As she progressed with her thinking, Young realised that there was more to learn about this syndrome and she spent a large part of her life dedicating herself to discovering more about it.

As you read this chapter, you might start to see how imposter syndrome is showing up in your own work or in your organisation. For example, you might be experiencing procrastination – not being able to get on with projects due to the worries of not doing it perfectly. You might notice other people flying under the radar, keeping their heads down in case they are found out.

Dr Young identified five distinct categories of how imposter syndrome can show up. I have added scorecards below each of these roles to highlight how courage fares against fear.

1. **The Perfectionist**

    These people really want to focus on 'how' something is done. They tend to set very high goals for themselves. If at any point they don't meet that goal, then they assign themselves the label of failure. Typically, a perfectionist will ruminate a lot and procrastination will be ever-present in their lives. They worry about every step of every project. A downside of this worry is not letting go or delegating to others to support them in their work. They might have the judgement of 'control freak' thrown at them or even label themselves in this way. Shame is a powerful emotion that underpins the perfectionist.

    Scorecard: Fear 1, Courage 0.

2. **The Expert**

    This is a version of the perfectionist; they are very concerned with 'what' and 'how much' they know or can do. There is a constant fear of being found out, of not knowing everything there is to know about something. Often experts will be people who are constantly seeking out new learnings as they are never satisfied with what they already know. Believing that they will never know everything, they fear being found out by colleagues. I have worked with people in my coaching practice who have been at the top of their field for many years but who still don't believe they know enough. Fear of failure and again pervasive feelings of shame underpin our experts.

Scorecard: Fear 2, Courage 0.

3. **The Soloist**

   They care a lot about 'who' completes a task. They rarely, if ever, ask for help. Without a clear understanding of why, they set themselves up as a 'lone ranger'. Any admission that they might need help brings on the feeling of failure, and they often chastise themselves: 'why can't I do this on my own?' These people will refuse help to prove their worth to the individual or company they are working for.

   Scorecard: Fear 3, Courage 0.

4. **The Natural Genius**

   These people really care about 'how' and 'when' something happens. They like to work fast and show their mastery of skills with ease. However, if they struggle to become competent at a subject they will often shut down. Hanging their heads in shame, they go inside and beat themselves up as failures and for not being good enough. The natural genius may often suffer with a fixed mindset and be set back by their struggles, choosing to give up rather than push through.

   Scorecard: Fear 4, Courage 0.

5. **The Super Person**

   They measure themselves against how many roles they can juggle and excel in. They want to be the best boss, parent, friend and colleague. They often think of themselves as not really measuring up to the 'real deals' and push themselves more and more, often suffering from overload. Not willing to let any of these balls slip, they can be inclined to put a huge amount of stress on themselves, not leaving time to reflect on what they have done. In my own life, I know that I can fit this profile of imposter. I want to be the best coach, trainer, parent and friend. I have had to get comfortable with these feelings of inadequacy, which stem from my childhood, and recognise when my work is good enough. I have had to re-learn how to pause and put in reflection time for myself in the form of creativity.

   Scorecard: Fear 5, Courage 0.

In the above examples, fear is beating courage time and time again. This goes on day in and day out in many organisations and especially for people-helping professionals.

So what to do about it?

Having some insight into these types of imposter syndrome helps you uncover what it is that is driving this behaviour.

Dr Young used these five different archetypes to help people identify which type was showing up most in their lives. I do think that understanding this can help an individual track back to where it might have shown up at early stages in their life. Working on your own, or with a coach or therapist, it is useful to take the learnings from these early experiences and then make choices about whether or not these are still necessary for us in our adult lives.

The other way to approach this is to start with the fears. These four questions, which come from the work of author Byron Katie,[19] might help you challenge the thoughts and beliefs behind the fears.

1. Is it true?
2. Can you absolutely know that it's true?
3. How do you react, what happens, when you believe that thought?
4. Who would you be without the thought?

The techniques that Dr Valerie Young and Byron Katie offer are the ones I have chosen to adopt for myself and share with others, because of their simplicity.

Earlier in this section I noted that women tend to have these feelings more than men. As a woman, I feel that I must acknowledge this could be another way that, sadly, the patriarchy has made us feel. A wonderful blog post by Ruchika Tulshyan and Jodi Ann Burey was published by HBR in 2021.[20] Have a read and see what you think: is this true for you?

I will also refer you to a wonderful speech given by Reshma Saujani[21] to the graduates of Smith College 2023. The speech debunks the notion of imposter syndrome as a way to keep women, in particular, working in fear.

There are elements of imposter syndrome that I see in the work I do with clients, both men and women. As with every issue that leaders face, it is key to look at it from all perspectives – race, identity, equity and psychological safety.

Courage and the body

As a Multiple Brain Integration (mBIT) practitioner[22] I believe that we can really get in touch with courage when we connect to our gut. Our gut actually starts at our lips and ends at our anus – that is a long journey. Our gut has more than 500 million neurons centred outside of the brain. The gut also houses our gut microbiome, a collection of good and bad bacteria that naturally live in our gut. There is significant research[23] that shows the huge impact of a healthy microbiome on our well-being. Not paying attention to our gut can really sap our courage.

A lack of courage can be seen in a variety of ways. For example, sometimes we cannot find the words to speak back to someone who is challenging us and so our courage fails in our mouth. Other times, we notice that tickle in our throat as we speak aloud in a meeting. Faced with fear, we can feel that our courage is ebbing as our gut churns and gurgles.

We might find ourselves in a state of rumination as we endlessly chew over ideas over and over again, never moving forward, never completing projects that might be very close to our hearts. So connecting to our gut is an essential way to connect with our courage. The quickest way is to breathe deeply right down into your lower gut; try some coherent breathing, which I offered as a method in activity 1 on

Curiosity. Quieten your body, stilling it in a safe and warm place. Ask your body a question, something that you want a different perspective on. Wait, and be patient – our gut doesn't have a language centre of its own. You could be rewarded with an image, a feeling or a sensation.

Speaking to our gut is very similar to getting in touch with our felt sense, but not the same. What is the felt sense? Dr Eugene Gendlin, in his 1978 book, 'Focusing',[24] describes the felt sense as: *'the body's sense of a particular problem or situation. A felt sense is not an emotion. (...) a felt sense is something you do not at first recognise, it is vague and murky. It feels meaningful, but not known. It is a body sense of meaning.'* Gendlin goes on to share a particular way of getting in touch with the felt sense through a process called Focusing. As an mBIT practitioner, I believe that the felt sense is a combination of our gut brain and our heart brain communicating with each other.

In your connection with your gut brain, what may be offered is a way forward, a new perspective on an old problem. If that comes up, the best thing to do is move.

Moving our body is the way that we can motivate ourselves towards a courageous act. In times of danger, our bodies naturally halt activities such as digestion, and push more oxygen and blood to our limbs to get us to safety. Using this knowledge, we can use the act of walking to motivate us to get into courageous action, whether that be intellectual, emotional, physical, social, moral or spiritual.

Returning to The Wizard of Oz, maybe that story was about a re-connection with our whole body. Our head is where our curiosity lies, our heart – compassion for others, and our gut is where our courage sits.

What difference does courage make to how I lead?

In thinking back to all the people-helping professionals I have worked with, I have created a pen portrait for a very common type of imposter syndrome. In my table overleaf, I show how Becki's imposter thoughts can be transformed by using *The Change Flywheel* model to 'motivate yourself'.

Becki's feelings may still wobble and the self-doubt might creep in. But she has taken steps to stop thinking like an imposter. Over time and with conscious choices she will be able to change the way she speaks to herself, and catch herself when the imposter takes over her mind. The next time she gets a job she could instead find herself saying: 'Well done, me!'

The work of the courageous leader is full of movement, growth and uncertainty but most of all motivation. Motivation is what turns courage into actions. These actions in themselves create motivation for others to take action too. If we can be courageous we will see proof of this: a motivated team who set about their work with a positive energy in their heart.

A courageous leader who acts on the conviction of their beliefs can inspire their team to take risks. Whilst team members won't know how things will unfold, they can trust they will be supported by the leader and the rest of the team.

Courage creates movement in an organisation. There is no standing still when you are striving to improve the impact you make on your customers, products or people. A courageous leader knows when to leave one project to focus on another. The systems and procedures already in place allow for that incremental growth to occur naturally to

The Change Flywheel

Original fearful thought	New courageous thought	Result
OMG, I've got the job! How did I do that? I really didn't expect to get it.	Well done you! You clearly prepared well. Pause, breathe and then celebrate.	Becki is starting off straight away confident in her abilities. She's not rushing into a negative thought spiral.
They must have had only a few people on their list. I was just in the right place at the right time. There clearly wasn't much competition.	Yes, it was a small field but they were keeping to the person specification. My experience met all their criteria. I gave clear and considered answers and shared my experience coherently.	Becki here celebrates her measured tone and the space she gave to answering the questions.
Can I do this? I bet everyone is waiting for me to fail, especially my team leader. She always has a nasty word to say about anything I do.	I can't wait to tell everyone and celebrate this new beginning. I'm a little anxious about my performance but that's okay. These thoughts will help keep me grounded.	Here she acknowledges that performance anxiety we all get with a new job.
I wonder if they will change their minds. Have I had the official offer letter yet? If I haven't had an email by noon tomorrow I'll send them one myself.	I'm going to send a thank you email now to tell them how much I am looking forward to joining their organisation.	Becki shows confidence in her new place on the team and the courage to trust them to follow their procedures in their own time.
Leading for me takes a lot of energy. I'm going to have to stock up on chocolate and coffee.	New learning can take up a lot of energy but I will make sure I have a good amount of rest each day.	Becki shows the courage to let go of old habits and build new ones to support her new job.

a project with teammates knowing what their role is. They have the autonomy to get on with their job without constant checking in with their team leader.

Being courageous allows you to reach for your higher purpose, whatever that might be.

For some of my clients, however, understanding their purpose can be a challenge.

By being courageous as a leader, we can normalise imposter syndrome and be open with our teammates when it happens to us. We can also remind them how well that particular thought strand is helping them motivate themselves.

Seth Godin[25] says:

'The distance from can to will keeps getting larger. You can connect, lead, see, speak, create, encourage, challenge and contribute. Will you?

The confusion kicks in when we become overwhelmed by all the things we can do, but can't find the time or the courage to actually commit and follow through.

In the face of all that choice, we often confuse can't and won't. One lets us off the hook, the other is a vivid reminder of our power to say yes if we choose.'

I love this line: '*a vivid reminder of our power to say yes if we choose.*' Keeping my choices linked to a higher purpose always helps me make a courageous choice.

CHANGE FLYWHEEL TAKEAWAYS

COURAGE – motivate yourself

- Which of the six types of courage are you most missing right now or is it more than one?

- Out of the five distinct characteristics of imposter syndrome, which one is defeating your courage?

- Motivation sits in our gut. How can you use movement to enhance your motivation?

- How do you keep your choices connected to your higher purpose and courage?

How can developing courage help me create my future self?

Take a deep breath, focus on your heart and breathe into your gut, the seat of our courage.

The following two activities are designed to uncover anything that might be holding you back from tapping into your motivation. So be brave, as even small steps can create surprisingly large results.

Activity 1: Identifying limiting beliefs

Time needed: half an hour

Aim: to start to see the limiting beliefs that might be holding you back.

A lack of courage is often underpinned by a belief that we hold about ourselves that is no longer true. This simple activity can help us uncover some of the beliefs that we have allowed ourselves to form, most of them stemming from our childhood. This activity is drawn from the work of Mark Manson,[26] an author who shares evidence-based life advice.

Find yourself a quiet spot in your office or home.

Turn off notifications on your phone.

If you know that you can get distracted from an activity, set yourself a 25-minute timer on your phone. When it rings, stop the activity and decide whether or not you want to stop or continue.

The Change Flywheel

Write down all the beliefs that you hold about yourself that you know are true.

....
....
....
....
....
....
....
....
....
....
....
....
....
....
....

Then ask yourself: what if I'm wrong? Be creative and think of a world where you are wrong about this belief.

....
....
....
....
....
....
....
....
....
....
....
....
....
....

Then ask yourself: how is this belief serving me?

Often these limiting beliefs serve a different purpose. My limiting belief about not being a 'good' writer held me back for many years. The stories, poems and ideas I had were firmly kept in my head. The belief was there to keep me in my comfort zone, working on what I knew I could do. I held an outdated notion that an author was someone special, with special powers, and that could not possibly be me. Who was I, the youngest in a family, wanting to be an author? That was a skill set aside for older people, wiser people, people more worthy than me. These deep-seated beliefs have taken a long time to shift and they periodically raise their head to whisper in my ear. They protect me from ridicule; by keeping me quiet they think that they are keeping me safe, but in reality they keep me frustrated. What is your limiting belief protecting you from?

....
....
....
....
....
....
....
....
....
....
....
....
....
....
....
....

The Change Flywheel

Now is the time to really get creative. Come up with as many ways as you can think of for why you might be wrong about each of your limiting beliefs. Try to come up with 3 to 5 reasons why that assumption might be wrong. By repeating these over and over again, you help your brain to make new neural pathways. When that limiting belief shows up again, it can quickly take another path. To help reset my own neural pathways, I have written consistently, tried a variety of times of the day and made a new habit of it. Over the years, I have written stories at school, weekly school newsletters, social media and blog posts, poems and short stories. They all show me that I am indeed a writer.

....
....
....
....
....
....
....
....
....
....
....
....
....
....
....
....
....
....
....
....
....

The final step in overcoming limiting beliefs is to test the new belief. This takes a bit of time and patience. Working with a coach or a trusted guide, you can test them out verbally and see how they land in the physical sensations you find in your body. A strong empowering belief will be met with a sense of rightness inside; you might find yourself nodding and agreeing with yourself.

When you are testing out your new ideas, keep a record of how you feel when you start to dismantle old beliefs. Where do you feel a difference in your body? I always feel a difference in my heart and in my gut. I breathe more deeply when the limiting beliefs dissipate and my fingers type much faster!

Activity 2: Planning a new physical habit

Time needed to plan: 1 hour

Aim: to make a new or renewed connection with your body.

We've examined the gut-brain connection with courage. In order to feel and be more courageous we need to be and feel physically energised. To maximise that feeling, decide to put a new physical habit into place. It might be a walk, a run or something else.

When you are working on developing this new physical habit to build courage, the key word is habit. Habit means doing something regularly and consistently.

The 4 questions over the page will help you identify and build new habits.

The Change Flywheel

1. What does regular mean for me in my life right now?

Assess whether you want to do this physical activity daily, weekly or monthly.

....
....
....
....
....
....
....

2. What time of the day works best for me?

First thing, lunchtime, or at the end of the day?

....
....
....
....
....
....
....

3. What is the optimum length of time for me to undertake this activity?

½ hour, 1 hour or more?

....
....
....
....
....
....

4. What is the minimum amount of equipment I need to start?

How can I make this equipment easily accessible when I need it?

....
....
....
....
....
....
....
....
....
....
....
....
....
....

This last question may take the longest to answer. This is the question that might lead you down a rabbit hole into procrastination. When doing physical activity your exercise kit is important, as you need to feel comfortable and protect parts of your body. I have heard too many stories of people who start a 'Couch to 5K',[27] for example, and then end up with knee and back problems due to wearing shoes that caused more damage than good.

Don't be put off by the equipment – shop wisely and go second-hand if necessary to avoid inflated costs to your new habit.

INTERVIEW WITH VIV GRANT

Viv is an executive coach, author and public speaker. She was one of the youngest headteachers in the country, turning around a failing school. She has successfully run her business, Integrity Coaching, for over fifteen years and has worked with hundreds of headteachers in the UK and abroad. Viv dedicates her work to supporting school leaders to find true fulfilment in all aspects of their work.

Introduction

A fellow headteacher put me in contact with Viv at a time when I found myself at a crossroads in my life. As soon as I met her I knew that she was someone special. She has a quiet and steely inner resolve and such a clear purpose with what she does; it was refreshing to meet a black woman showing up so strongly in the education world.

Working with Viv and one of her associates, I started my journey into coach training which subsequently led me to where I am now. If I hadn't met Viv, I may have ended up on a completely different path. Once I had qualified, I approached Viv to see if she would take me on as one of her associates. Although she did have an ex-head on her team, she didn't have a primary head. My intention at that time was to stay working as headteacher and also work as a coach. That wasn't to be and I finally moved into full-time coaching in 2018.

My association with Integrity Coaching has remained firm. Viv had confidence in me; she allowed me to grow and nurtured my potential, for which I am truly grateful. Working for this forward-thinking company has brought me so many opportunities. Whatever the future brings, I will cherish my work as an associate of theirs.

Five questions about your work and approach to life

Curiosity

In the words of Stephen Hawking: *'Remember to look up at the stars and not down at your feet. Try to make sense of what you see and wonder about what makes the universe exist.* ***Be curious.*** *And however difficult life may seem, there is always something you can do and succeed at.'*

How do you keep your curiosity alive in the work that you do today?

Viv's response was just as I expected. She responded with a question, and asked herself – *what am I learning to do more*? Her answer was to try to have an almost *'childlike response'* to life, to keep that innocent mindset that allows for a new approach. She reminded me of the piece I wrote in the section on curiosity, where I asked – what is curiosity?

Her desire to retain that innocence in her everyday life helps her in her work with clients. Keeping that curiosity alive enables Viv to accompany each client on their particular journey without making assumptions about what might be going on for them.

A childlike mindset has also supported her personally. Recently, she decided to learn to ride a bicycle. During the first lockdown, she also started to dabble in watercolours. She wants to be *'always on the edge of something new'*. This is the place where she is reminded of what is right in the world, not just what is wrong.

Viv has also started to learn to ride a horse, which she adores. As she engages with another living thing, there is a sense of adventure and 'not knowing' that occurs with every ride. Together she and the horse are helping regulate each other's nervous systems. Her current challenge is mastering the riding trot, perfectly synchronising her movements with the horse's.

By allowing that space of not knowing and getting into sync with her movements, Viv is allowing her body to learn to be in flow. It is not just our minds that need to learn to focus but our body-mind too. In flow, she then 'invites in that kind of mindset, that attitude, that way – in essence a sort of not knowing'.

Courage

It takes courage to be a leader. Thinking about the key leaders in your life, how did the courage they showed in their lives support you to be courageous in yours?

> *'Grant me the serenity to accept the things I cannot change, the courage to change the things I can and the wisdom to know the difference.'*
>
> **Reinhold Niebuhr**

As a starting point, Viv referred to this quote – one of her mother's favourites. Her mother was very ill at the time of recording this interview, close to death, and she had just shared with Viv that she was feeling accepting of this. Viv, at this late stage in her mother's life, was still learning about the things we can change. It takes courage to accept vulnerability, to know that you need help with dressing, washing etc., help that you didn't need for most of your life. Up to a year or so ago, her mother was – in Viv's words – the *'complete antithesis of vulnerability – she was strong, she was armed'*. In learning to embrace vulnerability, it has become her strength and has given Viv a greater insight into who her mum is.

It takes courage to accept and meet your needs right now.

The second person who inspired Viv was the headteacher of the school where she was a deputy and subsequently became head. This person, Irene, always saw the potential in others. Although not a coach, she behaved exactly as a coach would behave. Viv learned the art of being courageous from Irene, and the need to put ego to one side and understand that, as a school leader, there is a greater purpose at stake. She learnt to be humble and not see all issues from the point of view of *'what's in it for me?'* In retrospect, she was what is now known as a servant leader. She embodied the five distinct strengths of humility, listening, trust, caring and valuing people.

Viv recalled how Irene would push back against the dominant narrative at that time of hero leadership, particularly in education. It sounded to me, as Viv talked about Irene, that she was a woman who had patience too – patience and wisdom to know that not all of us show our true potential straight away, that potential comes with nurturing. This particular leader in Viv's life got a lot of pushback from governors and members of staff who wanted a more autocratic leader for their school. Viv has really embraced servant leadership – and the vulnerability she saw in her mum – in the way she leads her business today.

Now she works from a place deep within her. In fact, during the interview, she often placed her hand or hands near her heart. She talked about the work she does now as *'bringing out the gold'* in others. Many of the people who are drawn to working with Integrity Coaching are those who want to be better versions of themselves. In her work with school leaders, the people who ultimately benefit most are, of course, the children.

Creativity

In the words of the late great Sir Ken Robinson: *'I believe this passionately – that we don't grow into creativity; we grow out of it or rather we get educated out of it.'*

What advice would you give schools to help children develop their creative thinking?

'We need to re-educate our school leaders to think about what is the purpose of school education again?'

Perhaps, they may come to see that the way the system is at the moment is not set up to serve the child.

Currently, we have a very technical approach to education. The awe and wonder we should be nurturing in children has been replaced with measurement. How well are they doing?

Interview with Viv Grant

Are they (children) performing to expected standards? The key purpose of education has been forgotten.

Viv knows that this has been a key issue as she has education leaders coming to work with her who are so far removed from their purpose that they feel like giving up. They know they are perpetuating the system but don't know how to change it.

We had a short discussion about SATs and exams as both of us have children who have recently taken their A Levels. The way that schools approach the testing system can radically differ from one school to the next. Viv's child has been exposed to cramming and more cramming and is getting more and more stressed. My son's school had a different approach. They cultivated the group, taking the children away just before the exams to help them de-stress and remind them that no one needs to be alone.

That small gesture supports a viewpoint that I hope my own child – as well as the other students – will take into their future life.

Viv wants her clients to *'reconnect with their own school days. I think we need leaders to revisit what was positive and negative about their school life as we all lead from a personal space'*.

As school leaders, we can support new staff to reflect on these issues by using the questions recommended as part of the Warner Report published in 1992,[28] and which I used throughout my time as a headteacher. One of the questions that in particular gets people thinking:

What experiences, either in your childhood or adult life, led you to want to work with children/young people or their families?

Viv shared a piece of learning from another of her associates, Giles Barrow:

'He talks about the notion of selfhood. Between two individuals there is always an encounter. In that encounter, there is the possibility that each person will meet a version that they have never met of themselves before. This can only happen if at least one person has a strong sense of who they are. In terms of the teacher, "who they are and what they bring to the classroom".'

As educators, we need to ensure that we strive to work on getting to know ourselves. When we are working in a way that is not just putting on a show for others, we will really help the pupils connect with themselves too.

Viv spoke of a particularly poignant moment when her son shared some of his thoughts about school as he made his way to university:

He said that he had *'lost himself at school. He recognised that at school he could never be fully accepted for who you are and that you have to adapt in order to fit in'.*

He then told Viv: *'I don't want to do that anymore, I'm not going to be like that.'*

This question troubled Viv, as she realised through her answers that:

'What we are teaching our young people, whether explicitly or implicitly, is that it's not okay to be yourself. We might say the right things but we are not teaching them to be themselves.'

Community

For many years, I have had a postcard above my desk outlining '44 ways to build community'. What communities do you lead or have you led in the past, and what helped them grow?

'*I want to start with the Integrity community. I never imagined that it would be like it is now in terms of the associate team but also in terms of the number of headteachers and schools that we serve.*'

Viv has a huge community, a community that wants to follow her. Why? Not only does she have something valuable to say but she also says it with humility and love.

'*It feels like magic and a bit of a miracle.*'

Supporting Viv to give a bit more detail, I suggested to her that if it were magic, it needed some ingredients to make that spell. I believe that these ingredients are ones that all leaders should take note of.

'*Self-belief, be you, be authentic and vulnerable at the same time, choose similar partners with the similar vibration or energy to accompany you on your path.*'

Viv recognised that what helped her Integrity community to grow was sharing a similar purpose, recognising that we are, of course, all different but together we make a perfect jigsaw puzzle.

Reflecting on her growing associate team, Viv knows that each one of them brings something different to the table. It's rather like the DISC reports (personality profiling tool) that I use and Viv uses with clients: we all have each trait within us but some play more to one trait than another. The Integrity community continues to go from strength to strength.

Viv recalled another community that she built, that of her first school as headteacher. When she took over as head, this school was broken. It had a fractured structure born of racism in the community, a challenging Ofsted Inspection and staff that didn't want to be there anymore. What reconnected this school was the magic ingredient of love. This point took Viv right back to the last question about what schools need to do to develop creative thinking. She was keen to add to her previous answer that school leaders need to lead with love.

Viv shared several stories of children who had thrived under the love that she and her staff had provided at this school, children who now physically tower – head and shoulders – above her and who still talk about how Miss Grant loved them.

A child called Elliot couldn't say the words but showed it in a different way. Elliot was the child who tested her every single day. The last out of the car park on the day she said goodbye to the school, he came and hugged her without words. Sometimes we cannot put words to the way we feel, we can only use our bodies.

To build and maintain a successful community, you must return to the purpose of why you are doing this work in the first place.

Viv's purpose is to help others get in touch with their true self. Their true self is what their *'education has told them to shut off, that (education) has taught them to push behind'*.

'*What is it that schools seem to teach children that to be yourself is not enough?*' Viv believes that is because so many leaders don't know who they truly are.

Change

Change is the only constant in our lives or so the saying goes.

How do you keep harmony in your life and in your work?

As much as Viv loves her work, she also recognises that she needs to fulfil other areas of her life, hence the horse riding, bike riding and watercolours. She loves to spend time in nature and is lucky to be able to regularly escape the busy London life she leads.

Viv also puts a rhythm into her work; she shared one tip with me for how to start the day. She loves hula hooping – she gets up, puts on her favourite songs and hula hoops in the kitchen. She frees her spirit and simply focuses on the hoop and the music. She then closes her days with meditation. These rhythms and routines help her maintain harmony. They allow her time to think and get in touch with what's going on in her mind.

How does Viv embody my *Change Flywheel* coaching model?

Viv's questions help propel her forward. They create the momentum for her to make courageous decisions regarding her business and how she shows up as a business leader.

Her love of the arts supports her work, as she takes solace in the joy of painting and drawing. She seeks to stay true to her purpose of being vulnerable and authentic, and her energy is infectious. She models all of this so well within her coaching community, creating a magic that inspires others to take heart and move forward.

VIV'S TAKEAWAYS

Curiosity: What in your life needs that innocent childlike mindset right now?

Courage: Servant leadership embodies five distinct strengths of humility, listening, trust, caring and valuing people. Which of these strengths do you want to develop?

Creativity: How do you lead with love in your life?

Community: What three magic ingredients would you add to a recipe for community-making?

Change: How do you get your body-mind into the groove? Hula hooping, meditation or something else?

INTERVIEW WITH JEROME MING

Jerome is a photographer, artist and photojournalist who travelled extensively across the whole of South-East Asia. The images presented in his book, 'Oobanken', capture a time in his life when he lived in Yangon, Myanmar.

> 'Oobanken seems to be about a home, a house or a mix thereof – a subconscious outpouring of desires for domesticity or understanding of place if one is transient.'
>
> ASX website

Introduction

Jerome was an artist-in-residence working with Richard Layzell, whom I also interviewed. I worked with Jerome as a young teacher and I was keen to interview him as I knew this particular time in my life was transformational in the way I developed as a leader. Letting go, just being and watching things evolve was encapsulated in the House of Nations, the art project we worked on together. You can read about it in the section 'My Journey.'

Jerome joined Richard in supporting the work around the House of Nations. He captured the work of the children in beautiful photographs that perfectly expressed that moment in time. He continued to do this in his global work as a photojournalist and artist for the next 30 years.

Interview with Jerome Ming

Jerome's quiet presence and unique view of the world provide space for creation. He is an artist who does not make a distinction between a child's eye and an adult's eye. He sees them as the same and champions creative endeavour at any age.

Five questions about your work and approach to life

Curiosity

In the words of Stephen Hawking: *'Remember to look up at the stars and not down at your feet. Try to make sense of what you see and wonder about what makes the universe exist. Be **curious**. And however difficult life may seem, there is always something you can do and succeed at.'*

How do you keep your curiosity alive in the work that you do today?

'As an artist, I've never really questioned myself or considered it. To be an artist, I guess, to work in this way, you have got to be curious. I think it's about your environment, what's around you and also in terms of what you do, what materials are used, etc. There is photography – working with your hands and questioning the materials or how far you can go with those tools as well.'

Jerome talked about how he had moved from a long career in photojournalism to working on creating art related to how the world was engaging with him at particular moments in time. Travelling across South Asia, he was drawn to the points of history that his newspaper wanted him to capture. He later made a conscious decision to move out of journalism and his photography is now driven by a desire to connect with the world as an artist. While his previous work was about expressing a topical story and a worldview, it is now about expressing his own view of the world.

Jerome also talked about how it felt when he noticed his work was not as fulfilling as it had been.

'In a way, it was like my writing was off. It was not the right word, but I was using certain kinds of situations in my photography to explain what I was doing or trying to get involved in, or trying to say something about my experiences.

So there was a gradual shift inwards because the language I was using was not mine. I guess what I am trying to say is that it wasn't my voice or visual language that was unique to me. Photojournalism was a set language, a template of how I could convey images. So I set about using the medium to get an understanding of that medium in a different way.'

The birth of his daughter and her growing curiosity about the world served as an impetus for his artwork. He started capturing her early interactions with the world.

Initially living in Poland, then Ireland and later South Africa, Jerome realised that his daughter was living in a similar environment to the one he had experienced as a young child. She was having similar experiences to him, in terms of the quality of light and the unfamiliar sounds that she was exposed to. Now, living in Japan, she still remembers these early interactions with the world.

Courage

It takes courage to be a leader. Thinking about the key leaders in your life, how did their courage support you to be courageous in your life?

'I actually thought about Richard as he is someone you know. Richard has been a kind of mentor, but we don't have that relationship. I've known him for a long time. We have re-established contact. Richard has always been there in that sense. And I guess I see courage as someone who pursues the work they do or produces what they do. He has a label of a performance artist. He had written a book about performance using his tools and was probably one of the first performance artists.'

Jerome shared the effect that Richard's early performance artwork had on him. In those early days, performance artists worked in a space which was not clearly defined. People were not sure about what they were doing in the eighties and early nineties. Now there is a clearly defined space; there are events that people recognise and know and are part of our own experiences. For example, the Edinburgh Fringe Festival is a recognised place for performance art to feature.

There is a social approach to Jerome's work that communicates universal issues to a broader audience. He has another way of looking at issues.

I asked Jerome – how this different way supported him to take a different perspective on life?

'I guess that the work I do is not about thinking as an artist but thinking as a human being. Fundamentally, it is about being a human being and just relating to people in or communicating with people in a very particular language.

If you look at the leaders that we might put on a pedestal, they just have a particular way of communicating in a language that gets through. Good orators are good performers. Richard understands how to communicate with others.'

Jerome then went on to say that most of the writers and artists who have influenced him have been from the last century rather than the current one.

He found it hard to identify anyone else from his childhood or early years who may have shaped the direction he took as an adult. He talked about how he was never very good at anything academically. He felt that he was just *'okay'* at school. What he did know was that he had a stubborn streak that drove him to pursue a path as some kind of artist – although he had no clear idea of what kind.

He knew that he had to find a way to express himself. His parents supported him because they had no choice. Reading between the lines, it sounded as if he did not measure up to their expectations.

Creativity

In the words of the late great Sir Ken Robinson: *'I believe this passionately that we don't grow into creativity; we grow out of it or rather we get educated out of it.'*

What advice would you give schools to help children develop their creative thinking?

Jerome agrees that institutions stifle creativity. He can see that more and more, and now also with his daughter.

'She gets it ... she gets that when you mix colours, you make another colour. She gets particular shapes, and that if you do something in a particular way that you have an effect on something else. There are certain things that you don't need to teach her because it comes naturally.'

A school does have to be safe – there are things that need to be taught. But in terms of art, Jerome talked about having an environment to explore and maybe with adults not interfering as much as they do now, to give children an opportunity to express themselves in their own individual way. Jerome recognises that even when his own daughter was not able to speak, she was still communicating – observing and fully aware of what was going on.

He shared that he does not view children as children but as people. He talks to children as he would to an adult.

I agreed with this way of thinking as all too often, in my experience, adults in schools limit children by imposing a hierarchy on thoughts, such as particular ways of doing things. This is then magnified up through the system when those limitations then come from local and national governments.

Community

For many years, I have had a postcard above my desk outlining '44 ways to build community'. What communities do you lead or have you led in the past, and what helped them grow?

When answering this question, Jerome talked a lot about how he didn't consider himself to be part of any community apart from his small family group. The *'nomadic'* existence he experienced as a photojournalist and in his youth continue to shape his life. He shared that he and his family have moved every two years as his wife is a diplomat. But even in that movement, he recognised that there was something he gave to his community.

'An acceptance of sharing information, possibilities and in the end we try to help as much as possible, knowing that we are going to be moving on to something that will be different.'

Throughout Cambodia, China, Cameroon, South Africa, Poland and Myanmar, there are people he knows. He wasn't too sure what connects them.

Jerome talked about how he used his curiosity to support the few people he did meet or live with in these isolated diplomatic communities. In Cameroon, he lived in a compound community where the only person he talked to was the guard. He helped look after the goats there to support the community. In Myanmar, the only person he communicated with was the chauffeur who was chosen to drive his family.

Now in Japan, he still has a very small community – just his immediate family – and much of his day is concerned with supporting his daughter.

'I take her to school, I work in the studio, go and pick her up, make dinner – that's my day, that's been the case for five years.'

Jerome seems happy with this small community. It allows him time to get completely engrossed in his work. By allowing his community – in other words, his daughter – to grow, he avoids being distracted by too many people.

Change

Change is the only constant in our lives or so the saying goes. How do you keep harmony in your life or your work?

This was an easier question for Jerome. For many years he lived his life against this tenet.

'I am engaged with life and what I do with art as one. I didn't make a distinction. Life and art is one.'

'When I worked in photojournalism, I never knew what a weekend was, it was moulded into one. What was a holiday? Everything was so consuming, you never made distinctions.'

He recognised that the scheduling that was imposed by the fact he had to care for his daughter was good for him. Work had to have boundaries.

Jerome knows that what he is doing with his art is in its *'infancy in terms of output'*. Over the past 30 years, he has consolidated his practice and is now using what he has learnt to create art that is *'tangible and something new'*.

Jerome is committed to continuing to produce art and to not stopping.

Keeping on doing brings harmony to Jerome. A structured day supports him too and it is only because of his daughter that he truly recognises this element of harmony for him.

How does Jerome embody my *Change Flywheel* coaching model?

Jerome uses the medium of photography to illustrate his encounters with the world without judgement, a third eye on the world. His images support him to know more about himself. His courage is seen in the way he has carried on with those encounters in his travels by changing homes and jobs. Creativity enriches all aspects of his life, particularly his relationship with his daughter. His connections with participants on the edges of his artistic, photographic and diplomatic communities ensure that all are seen and no one disappears. Jerome has an easy connection with change as it is life for him.

JEROME'S TAKEAWAYS

Curiosity: *'In a way, it was like my writing was off.'* When is your work 'off', and what do you need to get it back 'on'?

Courage: Think of the groundbreaking leaders in your area of work. What characteristics do you admire in them? How have they influenced your work?

Creativity: *'There are certain things that you don't need to teach because it comes naturally.'* What comes naturally for you?

Community: When Jerome was living in Cameroon, he looked after goats. What small job do you do in your community that helps it run well?

Change: Jerome's mantra for his life can be read as an equation. Life + art = one. If you were to write your life and work as an equation what would you put in here: ? + ? = one.

CREATIVITY

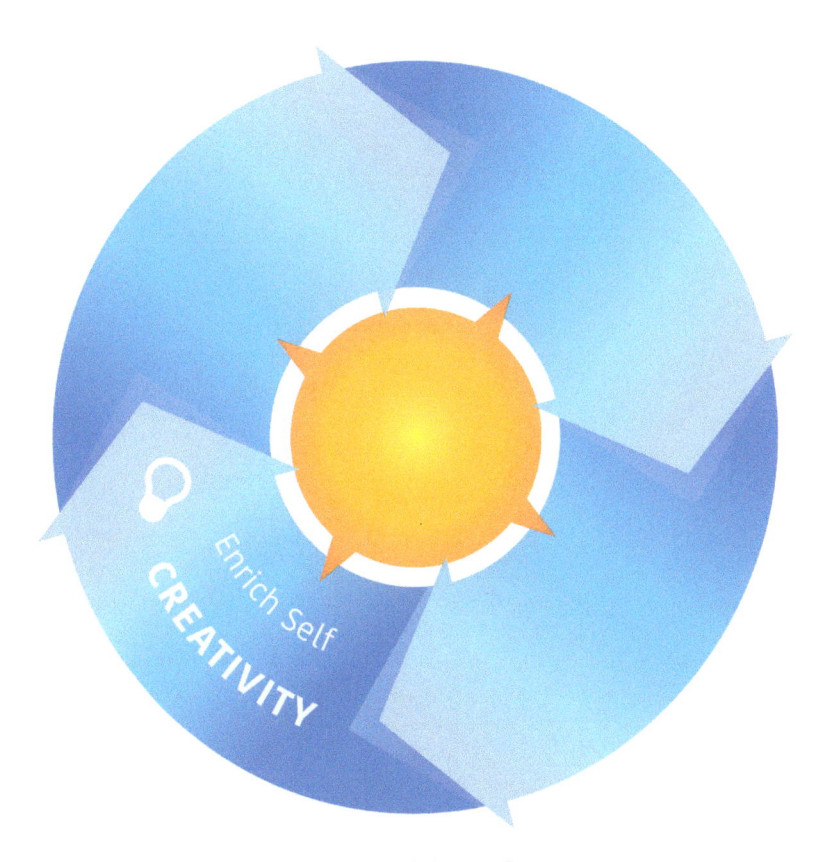

'You can't use up creativity. The more you use, the more you have.'

Maya Angelou

What is creativity?

Two refrains from a song featured in the film 'The Sound of Music' come to mind when I think of how to define creativity. When Maria is late for prayers, the other sisters and Abbess sing about how to solve a problem like Maria. They sing about the challenge of containing and catching the spirit of Maria, likening her to a cloud or a moonbeam.

Creativity feels ephemeral to me. Often elusive, it can come and go like a moonbeam or a cloud. That elusiveness and almost magical quality we associate with 'creatives' can keep many leaders steering away from creative endeavour. In my work as a coach, I see a few reasons for this. A lack of time, due to too many pressures, keeps leaders doing the same thing over and over again without progressing with their work. Doing too much and being too busy is a real block to creative thought. Fear of operating in a new way is also a challenge. It's so much easier to keep with the status quo than strike out on a new path.

Creativity can be defined in a very simple way. The Cambridge dictionary defines it as *'the ability to produce or use original and unusual ideas'*.

The Longman dictionary goes one step further, saying it is *'the ability to use your imagination to produce new ideas, make things etc'*.

Oh, that word – imagination. It can send many leaders running for the hills.

For many, imagination is something that is squashed out of them as children. Being told to 'pull your socks up' or 'stop daydreaming' are examples that come to mind for me.

Comments like this butt up against requests from others for leaders to think creatively under pressure.

So I am going with a definition from Sternberg and Lubart, [29] which describes creativity as the *'extraordinary result of ordinary processes'*.

Taking this further, my own definition of the creative process is *'the consistent process of learning through failure in the pursuit of extraordinary results from ordinary processes'*.

Some of us bridle and bristle when asked if we are creative. The word can evoke feelings of despair as we remember struggling to paint that picture in the very particular way our teachers set out for us, or to write that poem in the specific style of a poet we studied in class. The inventiveness aspect of the creative process was often forgotten in school in the effort to get content out of children. The joy and playfulness associated with creating get lost in the delivery of these ordinary processes.

In my own creative path, I have been reminded time and time again of the extraordinary results of ordinary processes. To write this book, I had to set out an ordinary process of showing up each week at a particular time to write. Over time, I had to adjust my writing habits many times to keep on track. I had to set a time each week to read and research, and to reflect on my coaching sessions in relation to my *Change Flywheel*.

For many years I was convinced that those authors, painters and musicians I loved had somehow mastered the art of alchemy, in the creative endeavours that came from their fingers and minds. Now I know that imagination and creative thought come through that consistent ordinary behaviour of creating on a regular basis. Consistency helps us be creative.

Underpinning the consistent behaviour I put into practice is the notion of time. I give time to being creative and I put a value on that time. My favourite quote from the Tao of Pooh[30] is that *'we cannot save time, we can only use it wisely'*. Maybe creatives are people who use time wisely – time spent on consistent processes that yield extraordinary results.

What time gives us is an opportunity to pause, ponder and percolate.

Creative ideas are just like my favourite tea, Rooibos; the flavour comes when it is left to percolate for a while. Creating under pressure is doable, but the best results come when you have time to think.

Take a pause here and percolate on those times when you have given yourself space to think about an issue or a question. What was the outcome? How has time enhanced your ideas and output? As leaders, how do you create that time to think?

'As strange as it sounds, creativity can become a habit', says creativity researcher Jonathan Plucker PhD, a psychology professor at Indiana University. *'Making it one, helps you become more productive.'*

Do you want to make creativity a new habit?

Here are some suggestions to support you in that process:

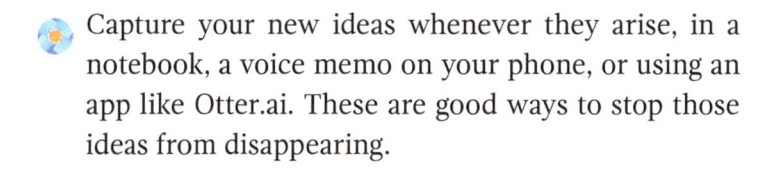

- Capture your new ideas whenever they arise, in a notebook, a voice memo on your phone, or using an app like Otter.ai. These are good ways to stop those ideas from disappearing.

The Change Flywheel

- Seek out challenging tasks. Take on projects that don't necessarily have an obvious or easy solution, such as how to get from A to Z without using Google Maps or maybe how to cook a meal for two with a maximum of five ingredients. Challenge your mind to come up with new ideas using your old knowledge.

- Broaden your knowledge. Yes, you might want to learn more about your area of expertise, but taking a class in something completely different can also support your current work. All these interconnected pieces of knowledge will find a way of connecting to create something novel and worthwhile.

- Surround yourself with interesting things and people. Varying the people you spend time with, or chatting to new people on the train or in a restaurant can all help generate diverse ideas that you can use to be more creative in the way you show up in the world. Creativity is a time to enrich ourselves.

- Look for connections between your work and home life. If you like gardening, can you get plant care into your working day? Create your own connections.

How did I make creativity a habit in my life?

As a headteacher with young children, I did not have any time for myself. Any downtime was spent napping in front of the TV, and there was a distinct lack of creative endeavour.

I was a headteacher, teacher, mother of two small children, wife, daughter and sister to many. But Sam – where was Sam? Speaking to fellow heads, I knew that this loss of self was very common. We shared our war stories at conferences and network sessions.

Many colleagues chose to work very long hours in a drive to stay on top of heavy workloads. Some expressed their relief at being able to be alone after school closed so they could 'get down to work'. In the daytime, they would be focused on connecting with the many people who worked in the school.

Many confidentially shared worries about putting a 'do not disturb' sign on the door in fear of staff disapproval. They all said they had no time for themselves and were exhausted.

For me, the turning point came as I stood in the kitchen of two artist friends in Honfleur, Normandy, where my eyes were drawn to the amazing set of colours before me. These were not in a painting but on a sweater: rust, orange and red with tiny flecks of sage green. One artist had knitted the jumper for the other and had also spun the wool and naturally dyed the yarn with plants from their garden.

That evening was the spark that re-lit the fire of creativity in me. I had always created, having grown up in the household of a dressmaker. But I had felt I couldn't afford the joy of 'me time' as I had all these other people and projects to worry about.

So the decision to take up knitting not only helped me reconnect with myself but also became my way of calming my mind at the end of a busy day. I decided to share my journey with my pupils at the school.

They listened and questioned me whilst I knitted my first cardigan after a 20-year hiatus. They gasped with 'oh no, miss' when I unravelled the front with its incorrect shaping and cheered when a pupil modelled the finished article. These assemblies encouraged them to be brave, curious and accept change while showing them how a community can provide support.

By involving the pupils in my world, I showed them that I was also human and that, like them, I needed rest time. I needed to be consistent when learning a new skill. And just like when they were learning to read, write and add up, once that skill was mastered a whole new world opened up.

I learnt to weather the narrow views of some – 'isn't knitting just for grannies?' In time, I was able to shake up some fixed mindsets about what headteachers do with their time. I am proud to have taught many people to knit, both young and old, and continue to encourage others to find that creative spark.

The impact on me was immense. Every day since, I have sought to live a creative life. By giving myself creative time, I have also had time to think and to consider new ideas.

Creating connected me with new communities outside of education, giving me a different perspective on issues inside the school. By joining writing, knitting and sewing groups, I continued with my own learning and this kept me connected to my pupils' experience.

This boosted my well-being and my resilience. I learnt a huge amount about who Sam is and what makes me tick. By standing up to the negative viewpoints of others I made some positive changes which supported me in navigating the stresses and strains of my role as a headteacher.

Why does creativity matter to us as humans?

If I could quickly teleport you to anywhere in the world to show you a great example of this, I would take you to a cave in South Africa, the Wonderwerk cave. Inside, archaeologists have unearthed artwork and simple tools used to create fire dating back to 1.8 million years ago – not 40,000 years, as previously thought.

Humans have a distinct advantage over other animals – the capacity for creative thought. This creative thought gave our ancestors the tools they needed to defend themselves and the means to map out and remember elements of their lives through paintings, carvings and etchings.

I can take my imagination back to a time when our ancestors used to prepare animal skins to be worn as clothing. In that soothing motion of hand and flint as they scraped away the fat, I wonder if they started to use their power of forethought to imagine a different use for this skin – perhaps as a shelter in the form of a tent?

In 2020 when the world experienced the first COVID lockdown, some people found that a narrowed environment helped their creative endeavours to blossom. Finding ourselves trapped in our homes, brains were given space to pause, ponder and percolate and – what a lot came out. In those safe spaces, with the virus locked out, some managed to re-engage with their imaginations.

Were you one of those who turned their hand to art for the first time? You may have been inspired by artists such as Grayson Perry. I was inspired to cook and turned my hand to sourdough. I was also inspired to finally crack crochet, hanging two crocheted rainbows in my window as a tribute to the NHS. My crochet skills developed apace, taking on a unique piece of art in the form of a 192-square blanket which mapped out the seasons of 2021. Even while stuck indoors, we were inspired to put our own particular stamp on the world.

Along with staying safe during a pandemic, we also had to rely on a limited set of resources. Driven by delays in shipping, certain things were in short supply and we were no longer able to just pop out to the shops. Scarcity enabled our minds to think carefully about what we wanted to do with our resources. I saw this in action with my eldest son, whose Foundation art year was blighted by lockdowns. The huge clay sculpture that he had planned for his final piece was not possible, as we did not have the space or resources to support this work. In the confines of his bedroom and our garden, he created his masterpiece in the form of a film, exploring elements of his Sri Lankan past along with other parts of him that he saw within. As he made use of all of his family to support his art, I was very much reminded of those ancient cave paintings where everyone joined in to share the hunting expeditions or to place their hands together, reminding each other of who they were.

It felt like a collective shout-out of 'I'm here' to the world. Our creations are a way of reminding ourselves that we were here and we do make a difference.

The collective shutting in for many of us also provided a time for creative thought about what we wanted to do with our lives and what was most important to us. As I write this, the world is still spinning with the reverberations of the pandemic in the form of what was dubbed 'the great resignation'. I prefer the term 'the great realisation'.

The space provided by creative endeavour allows us time to slow down and think. It's an opportunity for those ideas brewing in our subconscious to come up to the surface and be birthed into the world.

Sadly, when asked if we are creative, many of us will laugh and say something like 'me, oh no, I'm no artist', thinking that to be creative we need to inhabit the world of professional artists and musicians. Creativity doesn't need to be commercial or even shared with others; its purpose is for us to experience a valuable part of ourselves. I believe that we are all creative people; we just need the right conditions and mindset to allow it to grow.

Creativity and our bodies

For me, creativity starts in our heads but is seen through the creations we make with our hands. In my chapter on curiosity, I wrote about two channels of perception: interoception and proprioception. There is a third channel that we are all very familiar with – exteroception: sight, smell, taste, touch and sound. The centres for four of these senses are found on our faces, in our eyes, nose, ears and mouth, so it makes sense to start with our head.

A lovely way to get in touch with exteroception is to use a grounding mindful moment, such as relaxing in your chair or bed and taking in the world through your senses. What can you see, smell, touch, hear and taste as you sit for a moment or two? By orienteering yourself in this way, you give yourself time to take in what is around you, see the space you are in, think and make a plan.

The Change Flywheel

When I am out and about on my daily walks, I often play a game with myself to activate my power of sight. Setting myself a small challenge to spot red or blue berries, or different types of birds, I activate my reticular activating system which is found at the base of our brains. It has many functions, but a key one is to filter out unnecessary stimuli from the brain. By giving our brain a prompt, it might let that particular item in. When you have decided to look for something new, you might notice that thing popping up in all areas.

Light is an excellent way to get creative – for those who see, as well as some of those with visual impairment. From the way the light falls on a wall to the shade created by objects and shapes, I'm pretty sure we have all been stopped in our tracks by the glory of light in our lives. I look forward to autumn and winter mornings as this is the time when the sun creates a beautiful rectangle of light that is visible from my bed in the early mornings. I find this light incredibly comforting and in the boundaries of the shape, my mind comes up with some very creative ideas.

When we get into flow, those creative ideas can flow out like water from a tap, particularly when we get away from our routine.

Research has shown that getting out into nature is very good for our creative thinking. I have a hunch as to why that might be. I think it is connected to our unique human eyes that can perceive so many different shades of green. Our eyes have evolved to perceive green more than any other colour because this ability supported us when we moved to a diurnal (daytime) activity and helped us to spot different leaves, berries and fruits to eat. I believe the calming green and the stillness of trees allow for so much to come to the surface as we connect with other living things. So get out in nature every day to stimulate your creative endeavour.

As for the fifth sense, touch, I am sure you too sometimes find yourself drawn to using your hands when inspiration comes – to create through cooking, writing or making in some way. Head to hands, and often hand to mouth. Being creative feeds our mind, body and spirit.

What difference does being creative make to how I lead?

In thinking about the people-helping professionals I have worked with, I have created a pen portrait for a very common type of leader, one who lacks creativity. I have called her 'Caroline' in my table overleaf, and you might remember her from the introduction. Here I show you how Caroline's lack of creativity can be transformed by using *The Change Flywheel* model to 'enrich yourself'.

Caroline might struggle when too many processes and procedures are changed. But by leaning into getting creative with others, she will enhance her job satisfaction. There is an underlying sense that Caroline likes to micromanage. If she can let go and let others lead more, she will find that overdependence on her by others will diminish. This will allow her to engage with new challenges and learning, thus engaging her creative brain.

The Change Flywheel

Original constricted thought	New creative thought	Result
People need me and people rely on me. I show up every day ... if I don't, who will sort out the many projects I have on my plate?	I like new people joining the team. Each new person brings a different perspective to the table. There might even be an 'expert' who is ideally suited to a project I lead.	Caroline engages her curious mindset that allows her to be creative with her new team members.
My systems are perfect, if a little long-winded. If a job's worth doing, it's worth doing well.	I recognise that we can all get a bit staid in our processes and procedures. Just because they are right for me, doesn't mean they are the only way. I'm looking forward to learning a few new shortcuts.	Seeing her work with another person's eyes allows her to make some tweaks and enhance her processes.
I need my spreadsheets – it helps me keep track of what's going on. It also helps me keep the team on track.	My spreadsheets are getting a little unwieldy, with so many columns and pages. Maybe they keep me on track more than the team. That's an enriching thought!	Caroline recognises that she might be imposing her needs and preferences on her team. To also serve her team, she needs to start thinking more creatively.
If we do it my way then I know we won't miss anything. This is the most time-efficient way for me to lead my team. I have let the spreadsheet go on previous occasions but it has always ended in disaster.	Perhaps once in a while, a refresh is needed, particularly as our team regularly changes from year to year.	Creative thought around time efficiency makes sense with changing people and procedures. The disaster comes when we stick to an outdated plan.
Oh no, I'm going to have to ring home to let them know I'll be late again.	Oh great, I have bought back some time to give to creative rest. I know that gives me such a big boost mid-week.	Caroline now has a better work-life balance. Her creative pursuits fuel her attention to work.

Creativity

Allowing yourself to be creative as a leader opens up many new possibilities. The simple step of asking the question 'what if?' takes us out of the day-to-day and into a new future. Creative leaders are the ones we remark upon as being innovative and interesting, and we want to include their opinions in the mix.

Allowing ourselves time to think differently enhances the work that we do at all levels, from mundane paperwork to the connections we have with our clients.

Creativity typically comes out as one of the top skills for leaders across the public and private sectors, so it's clearly something to embrace rather than run away from.

Creative leaders also don't come up with ideas all on their own. They consider the work of others, be it through researching initial ideas or simply chatting with teammates. All ideas are born out of other ideas; they don't just fall like the apple from the tree. Isaac Newton's theory of gravity was built on past ideas and those of his peer group of scientists. Reading is a key attribute of creativity – both reading around an issue and reading for the sheer pleasure of it.

Creative leaders are needed today more than ever before if we are going to take leaps forward in reducing global warming and managing the tremendous challenge of our unfolding 'polycrisis'.[31] There was an IKEA advert in the eighties with the slogan: *'chuck out your chintz'*. The marketeers were hugely successful in persuading a generation to rebrand their homes in a minimalist style, so different to their parents' generation. The creative director of that campaign, Naresh Ramchandani, played on the aspirations of a generation of women who wanted to live a life unfettered by tradition and social norms.

The Change Flywheel

I am convinced that our creative leaders are the ones who can make wholesale positive change in sustainability. We need another Ramchandani to change attitudes in a very short space of time, not using fear to challenge our thinking, as that can result in a public backlash, but a new and different reality that is possible and acceptable for the general public.

The creative leaders in the world of sustainability are the ones who are showing people how to have a different relationship with the world's resources. They need to show us all that the leaders who recycle, reuse and renew existing resources are the ones to follow.

People-helping professionals can sometimes struggle to see the power they have within their hands. If we give ourselves time and space to reflect and gain perspective, we will find that we are much more creative than we think we are. That creativity often comes from the connections we make with each other. People-helping professionals are pretty good at working with others. In my own life, I have drawn on my connections to support school leaders in balancing work with the rest of their lives.

Remember what I wrote about the Wonderwerk caves? The artwork and tools that were created were made with others around. There was a collective creativity at work in that cave – a set of ordinary processes which yielded extraordinary results.

Pay attention to how you show up consistently for others and work on adding in more space to allow your creative thoughts to flourish.

CHANGE FLYWHEEL TAKEAWAYS

CREATIVITY – enrich yourself

- Remember my definition of creativity: 'the consistent process of learning through failure in the pursuit of extraordinary results from ordinary processes'. How do you get that consistency in your life?

- What creative habit can you choose to nurture?

- Getting out into nature is very good for our creative thinking. If you cannot get outside, then how can you bring the outside in?

- Be more childlike and ask yourself the question 'what if?' It takes us out of the day-to-day and into a new future.

How can developing creativity help me create my future self?

Baby steps are what are needed to break down the barriers to creative action. We don't get competent at any new skill overnight; it's consistent practice over time that leads to competency. A small step might be to luxuriate in playing with the simplest of materials: a piece of paper folded in many ways to create origami or a ball of wool slowly turning into a scarf. With a little practice every day, you will notice the power of this space to create.

Activity 1: Nurture a creative mind through daily journaling

Time needed: half an hour each day.

Aim: to provide your brain with a brain sweep to allow room for more creative thought.

Early-morning journaling has been practised for many years. In her book, The Artist's Way,[32] Julia Cameron dedicates a whole section to 'morning pages': three pages of longhand A4 where you just write whatever is in your mind. This tool is an opportunity to let your brain and body just release whatever is present for you. Whether you are feeling grumpy, excited, anxious, or happy – any emotion is welcome in these morning pages. Cameron sometimes refers to them as 'mourning pages; in Jungian terms, she calls it meeting your shadow and taking it out for a cup of coffee. You decide whether or not you want to keep the pages or destroy them. There are no rules as only you will see them.

I keep a notebook by my bed, as I find that as soon as I get up other stuff gets in the way. By writing in bed I can connect more with that liminal, in-between space between sleep and wakefulness.

Activity 2: Identify your own personal obstacles to being creative

Time needed: 1 hour for each section.

Aim: to identify what might be holding you back from being creative.

There are some key characteristics of creative people cited by Dr Munir Shuib, a linguistic expert and writer on creativity.[33] He believes, like I do, that creativity can be taught and learned. His work over the past two decades has revolved around teaching students to be more creative.

Shuib believes that there are five distinct traits of a creative person. Which of these do you have?

☐ They are risk-takers

☐ They dare to fail

☐ They are willing to be different and separate from others

☐ They choose to be divergent[34] and follow an alternative path

☐ They can be impulsive and fickle, changing their minds quite often

The Change Flywheel

Now, the interesting questions are the ones we put to ourselves when we find that we don't tick these boxes:

Risk: What is stopping me from taking risks?

How does that lack of risk-taking show up for me in my professional and personal life?

What scares me about taking risks?

Where does that fear come from?

Failing: What makes me want to get things right?

When did I last fail?

What was the impact of that failure on me and on others in my team?

Where did I learn that failure was a bad thing?

Different: What stops me from wanting to show my differences?

How can I be different in the job I do?

How can I show my differences in how I show up in the world?

Where did I learn that to be different was hard?

Divergent: What does divergent mean to me?

How can I be divergent in my work right now?

What experiences do I have of divergence that ended badly?

Where would divergence benefit a project that I am leading right now?

Impulsive: What does the word impulsive mean to me?

How open am I to changing my mind?

Which of my authority figures disapproved of impulsivity?

What are the positives of being open to change?

The time you spend on these activities will slowly and incrementally support you in drawing more creativity into your life.

INTERVIEW WITH INGRID FETELL LEE

Ingrid Fetell Lee is a designer, author and founder of the blog 'The Aesthetics of Joy'. She has been featured as an expert on design and joy by outlets such as The New York Times, Wired, PRI's Studio 360, CBC's Spark, and Fast Company, and her 2018 TED talk received a standing ovation. Ingrid's path was not a linear one. She followed the question of a tutor and that created her path.

Introduction

My first introduction to Ingrid came through a newspaper article in a Sunday supplement. I read about her ideas on joy and knew that this woman had something to say about a subject I really loved. Soon after, I watched her TED talk,[35] entitled 'Where joy hides and how to find it'. Her idea about the aesthetics of joy resonated with me so strongly that I had to watch it again. Ingrid had found a way to categorise the ephemeral and it worked. I joined her online community and found a word for an activity I had pursued since childhood – #joyspotting: looking for beauty in everyday occurrences, in nature and in my surroundings, and cherishing the almost magical qualities of life in all of its glory.

I had the pleasure of meeting Ingrid on her UK book tour and felt very strongly that she was a woman of substance, a woman who truly lived her work. Ingrid has had a profound impact on the way I live my life and I was very grateful that she agreed to be interviewed.

Interview with Ingrid Fetell Lee

Five questions about your work and approach to life

Curiosity

In the words of Stephen Hawking: *'Remember to look up at the stars and not down at your feet. Try to make sense of what you see and wonder about what makes the universe exist. Be **curious**. And however difficult life may seem, there is always something you can do and succeed at.'*

How do you keep your curiosity alive in the work that you do today?

'I chose to study an intersection between two fields – design on one hand and joy on the other, which is – you know – part-emotional affective science.'

In looking for the intersection between different disciplines, Ingrid meant that she can never really master any one subject. These disciplines are wide and varied, including evolutionary psychology which investigates our preferences, affective science which has to do with our emotions, and positive psychology which is a branch of science that works on how we thrive, maintain positive mental health and overcome threats.

The constant moving between intersections supports Ingrid in keeping those new discoveries fresh in her mind: *'Living in this intersection is fascinating because it is always dynamic.'*

I could feel the energy as she talked: *'There's always another piece of research you could open up.'* This desire to learn, a key pillar of resilience, is unshakeable in Ingrid.

Ingrid loves *'living for the questions as opposed to living for the answers'*. As a respected designer and author, she is often asked for career advice by others. Her response to questions like Should I take this job? or Should I not take this job? is illuminating.

'I always say, are there interesting questions in the role you are in right now? And if there aren't interesting questions, that might be a good time to move on.'

It strikes me that if we all try to follow questions rather than answers, we might find ourselves leading more fulfilling lives.

Following questions has helped Ingrid make firm decisions about what she wants to do in her life. She gave an interesting example of this: her agent had suggested she start thinking about writing another book, but she found that those questions were not *'burning'*. If she was going to be true to herself and her curiosity, the questions would need to be *'burning'* enough to carry her through a whole book.

I wondered whether Ingrid's questions were linked to passion. The word she used was *'absorbing'*. She wants to get lost in the question. She said that these questions need to pull you in and might show up at surprising times, such as when you are in the shower.

Courage

It takes courage to be a leader. Thinking about the key leaders in your life, how did the courage they showed support you to be courageous in your life?

'The manifestation of courage is the courage to live your values and to stick to your values, even if the client wants something different, or your audience wants something different.'

Ingrid talked about the pressures that we all live with, in the world, particularly the pressure we get from social media to speak or not speak on certain topics. She navigates this territory by asking herself these questions:

What kind of world do I want to create?

What kind of world do I want to live in?

And how do my actions affirm that?

I think these are three very powerful questions that would be helpful to so many.

A professor in graduate school helped Ingrid hone these questions as he brought values into their conversations around designing and making.

'He used to say this thing – you have to earn your spot in the landfill.'

Ingrid went on to explain that when you design or make anything it is out of tangible matter. We all know that there is no bottomless pit that matter goes into on our planet. Discarded items end up in the ocean or in a hole in the ground. So if we are all to make more stuff it has to earn its place to exist. This knowledge helps Ingrid make decisions about what she designs. *'Is this really good for the world? Do I want to live in a world where this thing exists?'* These questions can challenge a designer as you are always supporting the client as well. But ultimately we are all responsible not just to ourselves and our clients but to the whole of the planet.

Her professor's questions helped Ingrid make socially responsible decisions about who she worked with. She does believe that it gets easier with age as this gives you the experience to draw on to help you recognise when to say no. I believe if we all used the 17 United Nations Social Development Goals to support our work, that would also help less experienced people make good decisions about what they make and do.

Creativity

In the words of the late great Sir Ken Robinson: *'I believe this passionately – that we don't grow into creativity; we grow out of it or rather we get educated out of it.'*

What advice would you give schools to help children develop their creative thinking?

'*I think the loss of physicality is the loss of creativity.*'

Ingrid reminded me of the danger of education, in that the older we get the more abstract it becomes. In her work on the aesthetics of joy, she explained that we lose joy when we lose our creativity and that can sometimes come with the ageing process. This resonated for me, as I know from my work with leaders that they mourn the loss of creativity as they become increasingly disconnected from their bodies.

For Ingrid, this shows up in writing. All too often we want to know what we are writing, but, she says, '*the reality is that writing is a process of figuring out what you want to say.*' The same principle can be applied to any creative process. Ingrid shared how her young son gets started with his painting. He has no idea what he wants to paint before he paints. He talks to the colours in a particular way that shapes the work:

'*Come on orange, I want to see you*'. Or '*Come on blue, I want to see you*'.

He talks to the colours as if they were his friends coming to play on the paper, and that's how his art gets made. He allows for space and he encourages his own creativity to emerge in the doing, in the process.

Community

For many years, I have had a postcard above my desk outlining '44 ways to build community'. What communities do you lead or have you led in the past, and what helped them grow?

Ingrid leads a large community called the 'The Joyspotters Society", for people who create joy. They may be affiliated through her blog or through a Facebook or Instagram group, and she has learnt to keep the community focused on joy.

Communities need boundaries, so encouraging positivity keeps these communities thriving.

Sticking to her values has also helped. Being transparent and open supports people to make the decision whether or not to stay in the community. One of the values that she and her moderators stick to is – no judgement.

'Judgement is the fundamental enemy of joy.'

This can be tricky to stick to but it helps differentiate facts from opinions. We all know those judgmental opinions that can take positive joyful energy to negative stress in milliseconds. Her communities are in the many thousands. At the time of writing this piece, Ingrid's Instagram community had over 63,000 members. That's a lot of joy and potentially a lot of judgement.

What also helps her communities grow is authenticity. She brings her whole self to the community. She talks about issues that are meaningful to her and in doing so touches the lives of many. A recent piece on breastfeeding has been commented upon many times and has been helpful to many. Being vulnerable in these interactions with others helps others see the whole person, not just a glossy cover page version.

Change

Change is the only constant in our lives, or so the saying goes. How do you keep harmony in your life or in your work?

For Ingrid, making the move out of the city and into the country has really helped keep harmony alive. The constant busyness of city life meant that Ingrid and her family were being moved further and further away from the things that brought them joy.

Daily routines like a walk or making a trip to the ocean give her harmony. She described the Atlantic Ocean at its most powerful: *'pounding waves, big surf swells and sometimes dolphins to watch.'* At least three of the aesthetics of joy are encapsulated in those journeys – energy, freedom and surprise, as well as a healthy dose of awe and wonder.

She loves to spend a lot of time with her family and, most definitely, outside. Ingrid talked about the joy she gets from a twice-weekly visit to a CSA. In the US, CSAs (Community Supported Agriculture) are places where people can go and pick their own vegetables and see how things grow. As a family, carving out time to go – rain or shine – is very grounding for them:

'The rhythm of being tied to a community, the intimacy of it, seeing the same people every week. It's a really special space.'

Ingrid, like me, is blessed with an ability to savour the seasons in all their glory. This activity supports her young child to connect with the seasons, to know and feel the cycles of life and growth.

How does Ingrid embody my *Change Flywheel* coaching model?

The energy in the intersections of life drives her curiosity to discover more about how we can be in harmony with the world around us and know our place in it. I love the courage she shows to connect her work with the future; that sense of generous spirit keeps her motivated. Ingrid clearly oozes creativity and her interactions with her child give so much hope for an enriched world. The 'joyspotting' community is one that does look for the positive but doesn't ignore the challenges. The constant companion of the natural world keeps Ingrid grounded and sure of the work she is doing to build a future inspired by the question, 'what if'?

INGRID'S TAKEAWAYS

Curiosity: What question is absorbing your thoughts right now? Capture it, let it flow through you and in you and see where it takes you.

Courage: What kind of world do I want to create? What kind of world do I want to live in? And how do my actions affirm that? Take a piece of paper and spend ten minutes answering these questions.

Creativity: *'Come on blue, I want to see you.'* What needs coaxing out in our life? If it were a small child or gentle animal, how would you get it to shine?

Community: *'Judgement is the enemy of joy.'* Where is judgement showing up in the communities you lead? What boundary do you need to put in place to keep joy alive?

Change: Take a look out of your window. What season is it now? How can you make contact with that season in a positive way?

INTERVIEW WITH LUCY SCOTT-ASHE

Now retired, Lucy is a teacher and headteacher, who worked in the South West and in London. She is someone who understands the mind of a child and has contributed to a book on children's writing.

Introduction

I arranged to talk with Lucy Scott Ashe the day she visited the Horniman Museum[36] with two of her grandchildren. She was filled with the joy of being a grandparent. For those of my readers who do not know the Horniman museum, here are Lucy's words: *'You will enter a world of curiosity and creativity'*.

Lucy was the second headteacher that I worked for as a young teacher. She joined as the deputy head when I was in my second year of teaching. Sadly, at the end of that year, the headteacher who was retiring passed away suddenly from a stroke.

Lucy was the most unconventional headteacher that I had ever had the pleasure of working with. What set her apart was her natural instinct to follow her heart. She did not conform to the stereotypical pressures on senior leaders at that time. Suits and twinsets were not for her; Lucy preferred to turn up to work in bright leggings and tee shirts. Her aesthetic definitely had an impact on my professional dress, and from that time on my choice was always bright tights and vintage cashmere.

Lucy remained headteacher at the school for six years and then left London to work as a head in Bristol. Her extensive experience in the world of children's writing was embedded in her leadership style. There was always a focus on freedom of expression.

Connecting with Lucy after many years felt timely and important. We picked up from where we had left off many years ago, and on hearing her responses to my questions I reminded myself why I still held her in such high esteem.

Curiosity

In the words of Stephen Hawking: *'Remember to look up at the stars and not down at your feet. Try to make sense of what you see and wonder about what makes the universe exist.* ***Be curious.*** *And however difficult life may seem, there is always something you can do and succeed at.'*

How do you keep your curiosity alive in the work that you do today?

Her first response was a true Lucy:

'Playing with the grandchildren – it is easy to be curious with them, especially as I am not in charge of all of them.'

Lucy talked about how she can quickly connect with and follow her grandchildren's thinking and interests. She finds this less easy with adults, though, and in recent years has become more tribal in her connections. Lucy was very much anti-Brexit and recognised that she can be drawn into one view over another. As a result of the *'political shenanigans'* she saw going on, she admitted to having become slightly less curious as to what goes on for adults. She recognised that she can want to win the argument and has to remember to be imaginative with people and keep an open mind.

Lucy was a headteacher for a total of 18 years in several schools. As a leader, she maintained her curiosity by not being dictatorial about how things were done. She enabled staff to create an open liberal curriculum, with a cross-curricular approach. Her aim was always to make sure the curriculum was culturally inclusive. Her time in an EAZ[37] school in Bristol gave her the flexibility of being able to go '*off piste*', in order to engage the imagination of the children who found school a challenge.

Lucy recalled how the school used the history of Bristol to connect with the children, exploring the links between the city and the slave trade. The teachers remained as hands-off as possible, allowing the children to lead the way. By not putting a particular destination on the journey a rich zigzag occurred. The interests of the staff also came into play and one teacher in particular went on to design a fully integrated curriculum. This person now works for English Heritage and is employing a similar format to the work that they do to enlighten their visitors.

To sum up Lucy's approach to curiosity in a few words – to have few boundaries; to link the learning to real-life issues; to be fully present; to bring in your own interests; and, to listen carefully to what the children are saying.

'*Life is full of possibilities if you allow it,*' Lucy said. She also expressed caution about the need to take breaks – a point I will pick up again later on in our interview.

Courage

It takes courage to be a leader. Thinking about the key leaders in your life – how did the courage they demonstrated in their life support you to be courageous in yours?

Claire Chappell was a key leader in Lucy's life. I had an inkling that this name would come up in our conversation about courage. You see, Claire Chappell was also a key leader in mine. I didn't know until this interview exactly how much of an impact Claire had on Lucy.

Lucy spoke about Claire as an exceptional person. Claire was Lucy's coach and she had worked as a counsellor. She taught Lucy how to stand up to the local authority, and how to phrase her responses.

'The whole point of coaching is to hear the other person and enable them to validate what they think and then have the courage to do it. Her open-ended questioning helped you to realise and take responsibility for yourself.'

Lucy originally went to work with Claire when she took over as a headteacher. Remember – she stepped into the role in very challenging circumstances. The previous headteacher had died just before she was due to retire.

'People were telling me all sorts of stuff and I felt overwhelmed. From these sessions, I was able to question in an open-ended way not in a closed way. I worked that way with children in particular. When you experience it yourself you get better at doing it. There was so much change in the school, it helped me to think out of the box in the school.'

In my own opinion, I think Lucy's courage was shown in the way she worked with leaders in the early nineties, encouraging them to be themselves – not to be swayed by others, but to learn to listen to their heart.

Lucy then discussed a teacher in her next school:

'She taught like no one else I had ever seen ... in the most creative way. She completely understood how a child learned.'

This inspirational teacher supported Lucy in developing the school in the educational action zone. Having someone like this who has faith in the vision, helps build more courage to follow your gut.

Throughout her career, Lucy has always been courageous: in her work with refugees, both children and adults, by being a stepmother to four and now as a grandmother.

Creativity

In the words of the late great Sir Ken Robinson: *'I believe this passionately – that we don't grow into creativity; we grow out of it or rather we get educated out of it.'*

What advice would you give schools to help children develop their creative thinking?

'Schools will help children develop creative thinking by providing a good curriculum that is meaningful to both the teacher and pupils. Teachers need to teach things that they are interested in. Children will develop creative thinking by having carefully crafted methods of teaching with open-ended solutions, an ethos that helps them develop personal skills.'

As a head, Lucy had to nurture staff who were willing to take risks, particularly in a climate where courage was wavering with the drive to increase SAT[38] results. She made the conscious choice to train staff to be risk-takers along with being resilient, and able to face personal and professional setbacks.

You will read more about Lucy's creativity in the section 'My Journey'.

Community

For many years, I have had a postcard above my desk listing 44 ways to build community. What communities do you lead or have you led in the past, and what helped them grow?

'It's about valuing all the people, allowing them to connect and not placing one above the other, no hierarchy, encouragement and accepting the differences and valuing the difference.'

I have set out above the many ways in which Lucy developed thriving communities in her professional life. Community building is still part of her life outside school. She lives on a terrace in Bath where there is active encouragement from the community to connect with each other. The community has created an ethos which brings people together in an encouraging and accepting way, whatever their differences.

That trust, which was fundamental to the way she worked, now shines through in her community work. Lucy supports a charity that plants up the gardens of people who are refugees in this country. She leads the gardening team in an effort to give back to her community. Linking in with her love of gardening, she is able to bring beauty to others who face rejection from so many. She believes the small act of planting flowers and vegetables can help grow new friendships.

'It was interesting. I began working with refugees at St. James school and now I'm working with them to help them develop their gardens. It has been a good full-circle activity.'

Trust and openness are fundamental to building community. When the ethos is promoted as a trustworthy one, people will want to belong.

Change

Change is the only constant in our lives – or so the saying goes. How do you keep harmony in your life and in your work?

'I try not to read the news.'

Lucy spoke about her life as a retired person who feels well-integrated within her local community. She told me that she is circumspect with her attention to the news, and tries not to get caught up in the minutiae of current affairs and politics. She aims to go for the long view – to live her truth and stick to it.

She is more accepting of change in her relationships but struggles with the political changes she sees in the world.

Lucy truly believes that we need to bring up our men in a different way and feels like there is a long way to go in this area. She spoke about her view that these changes in the world have meant that many men do not feel as comfortable in their masculine roles now and that we need to change how we bring up our young men.

Lucy aims to live her life in the present. Her daily practice of walking with two or three neighbours, sun or rain, is an important support to her. Friendship helps her be present.

The Change Flywheel

Along with those daily walks, Lucy spends a lot of time reading and being out in nature. She does consider herself to be too busy from time to time, however, and would like to strip back some of her activities.

How does Lucy embody my *Change Flywheel* coaching model?

By getting a daily dose of play in your life you will find out more about the world. Lucy embodies that childlike innocence to discover more. Her choice to stand firm and stand up for communities that don't have as much as others really embodies courage. Her love of open-ended questions that are born out of curiosity also sparks her creativity. Lucy is someone in my life whose answers really showed how much she is inhabiting the present. Her future is now and she relishes every minute.

LUCY'S TAKEAWAYS

Curiosity: *'Life is full of possibilities if you allow it.'* When were you more open in your life?

Courage: *'There was so much change in the school it helped me to think out of the box in the school.'* When was the last time you thought and acted out of the box?

Creativity: *'Teachers need to teach things that they are interested in if possible.'* What are you interested in right now outside of your work?

Community: Lucy is able to bring beauty to others who face rejection from many. What communities or people do you support who may have been rejected by society?

Change: Lucy aims to go for the long view, to live her truth and stick to it. What daily practices do you have in order to honour your values?

COMMUNITY

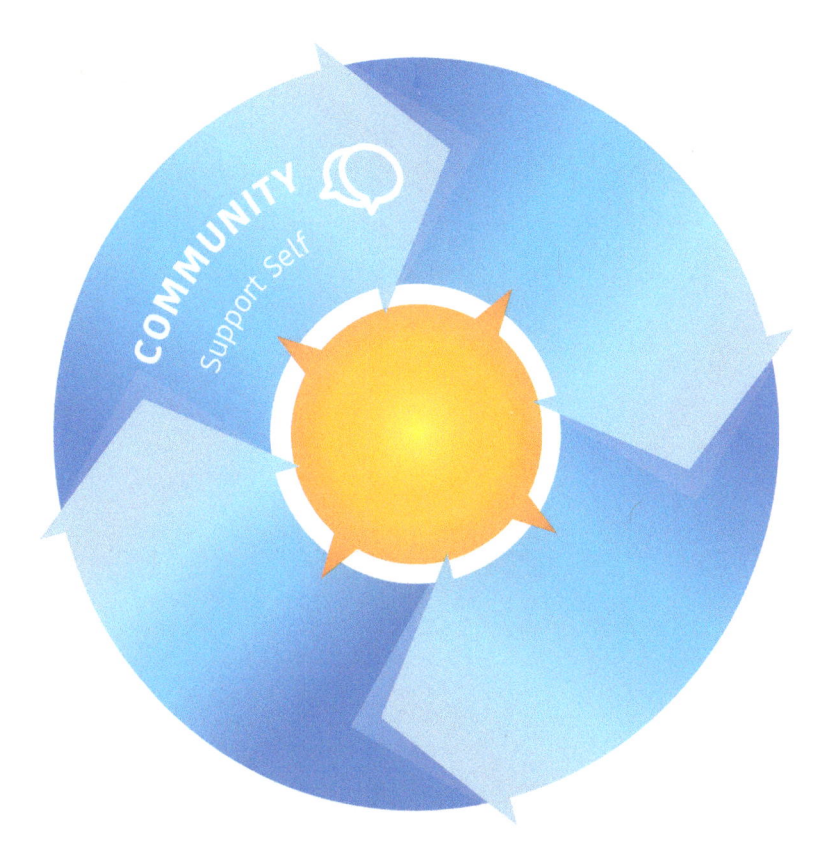

'Because it is not merely about surrounding myself with people who treat me well. It's also about surrounding myself with people whose self-worth, self-respect and values inspire me to elevate my own behaviour.'

Shonda Rhimes

What is community?

Family, friends and colleagues – the one thing these words have in common is people. Community is about others: it is about connection.

The Oxford dictionary says community is *'a group of people living in the same place or having a particular characteristic in common'*. It also talks of a feeling of fellowship, as a result of sharing common interests and goals. The root of the word is found in the late 14th century, denoting a common oneness that holds a group of people together.

That commonality can be experienced in a few different ways.

Our families are our first communities. Our very first experience of this starts in the womb where we commune with our mothers as we grow. This early partnership, which supports the life we were given by our father and mother, binds us with our ancestral community.

In the book 'A General Theory of Love,'[39] the authors delve into the deep limbic connection that a mother has with her child, that early earthy bond of two limbic brains that subconsciously feel each other. We absorb so much in utero, this small community of two, connected to our mother and feeling her emotions as she nurtures us inside.

'Bathed for months in (their) mother's vocalisations, a baby's brain begins to decode and store them, not just the speaker's tone but her language patterns. Once born, a baby orients to the familiar sounds of his mother's voice and her mother's tongue and favours them over any other. In doing so, (they) demonstrate the nascent traces of both attachment and memory.'[40]

Our families are the first naturally organised communities that we belong to. Whether we choose to stay in them is a decision for our adult selves to make. The desire to stay or not stay, however, is held deep within our limbic brains.

A key to staying connected is outlined beautifully in this quote:

'Being well regulated in relatedness is the deeply gratifying state that people seek ceaselessly in romance, religions and cults; in husbands and wives, pets, softball teams, bowling leagues and a thousand other features of human life driven by the thirst for sustaining affiliations. In early life, limbic regulation is not simply pleasure; it is also crucial training.'[41]

Moving away from our families as we grow older, another marker of community is locality. Although people moved around, they tended to do it in groups. The safety of the pack provided security for their families. We know this through historical studies of the movement of groups as they navigated the world, be that by land or sea and now by air.

In our digital age, locality is no longer as necessary, as we have created huge global communities that break down the barrier of land to bring people together.

All these communities, whether digital or in person, are often held together by a common belief or sentiment. For example, I belong to a few knitting communities: I have several local community groups close to my home and a city-based community group in my part of the UK. I belong to a national community group that occasionally meets up in person at knitting shows and exhibitions, and a global community group in the form of Ravelry,[42] an online knitting community where I can meet virtually with knitters from around the world. The common theme is a love of knitting and yarn. A piece of string is binding me to these people.

My knitting communities were naturally formed, born out of a desire to share patterns, give or seek advice, and share the joy of knitting. Communities can self-organise; they can grow spontaneously.

The common traits of communities, therefore, are that (1) they are made up of people, often held together by a common belief and that (2) they are self-forming. Locality may feature as part of the group but is not necessarily so in this digital age.

So what is it that holds and keeps us in a community?

What binds us is buried deep within us. If we feel regulated and resourced by a community, we are more likely to want to stay in it.

Both personally and professionally, I thrive on communities that regulate me and also make me think. I flourish in communities that share similar values and show me a way of living those values with a new slant. For me, these shared values are about being curious, courageous and creative, while knowing the value of connection and embracing change. The word 'elevation' in the quote at the beginning of this chapter immediately gives me the feeling of lightness, calmness and clarity. It's a way of being I strive for every day in both work and play.

It is the opposite of the types of community I tend to move away from. I don't want to be part of a community that never questions what I do. That's the path to becoming the emperor who wears no clothes. You might see this in the 'yes' people who often surround toxic leaders whose unthinking comments never get publicly challenged. If those comments are challenged, their own community will rear up and fight those challenges with more tissue-paper lies that everyone can see through but no one is courageous enough to tear down. I prefer to be part of a community that provides challenges that make me think, and where this is done in an empathic way that doesn't shut me down.

We stay in communities where we are seen and heard, where efforts and achievements are marked, recognised and celebrated. For many of the people-helping professionals I have worked with over the years, unsolicited criticism and lack of recognition can lead to deep frustration and resentment. In turn, this often leads to them leaving communities, meaning their experience is lost to the wider group they serve.

Why does community matter to us as humans?

Community is fundamental to humans and is, in fact, a matter of life or death.

People who do not have a community around them greatly increase their risk of early death. Loneliness is likely to increase your risk of death by 26%,[43] according to research by Holt-Lunstad from 2015. None of us needs to be lonely, there are billions of us after all. Yet research found that 3.3 million people living in Britain were 'chronically lonely' between December 2021 and February 2022. Loneliness has a hugely negative impact on humans' mental and physical well-being.

Robin Hewings, Programme Director of the Campaign to End Loneliness[44] said:

> 'Chronic loneliness is particularly difficult to move on from. It stops some of our most vulnerable people living life to the full and damages both physical and mental health. 'Levelling up', needs to include tackling loneliness and connecting most of the loneliest people in our society with targeted support.'

Why do we need this connection with others? To answer that question we need to turn to the work of John Bowlby, a British psychologist who was one of the first to discuss attachment theory.

Bowlby says that attachment is the *'lasting psychological connectedness between human beings'*. His work revolved around the development of stress and anxiety he saw in young children, particularly when they were separated from their parents.

Psychologists before Bowlby decided that this behaviour was just learned behaviour based on a negative relationship between the parent figure and child, and based on feeding. When the child gets nourished the attention-seeking behaviour ceases to be. Bowlby thought differently. He thought it wasn't about the nourishment of the body but the comfort and care that the child got from their parent figure – the emotional regulation that I mentioned above.

Attachment is therefore the emotional bond with another, which starts in utero with the baby listening to the mother's internal organs, breath and voice and sensing her emotional reactions to people and events in her life. This attachment is needed for a child's survival outside of the womb. The availability of the parent to give that care and comfort creates a secure base for the child.

As we move to adulthood, we still need those secure bases. We still need that care and comfort in our lives. The way that families now live mostly separately from their elders means that our elders are feeling increasingly lost and lonely. Over half a million people in the UK go at least five days a week without seeing anyone at all.[45]

We were born to be part of a pack and when separated from it, loneliness can be a killer.

Living in the digital age has made our children more lonely too. In a survey by Action for Children,[46] 43% of young people aged between 17 and 25 said that they experienced problems with loneliness, with many feeling unloved.

So what has this got to do with leading?

Well, we are all the leaders of our own lives. If such a large percentage of us suffer from loneliness we may find that it is hard to connect with the people around us. We have to be intentional and mindful to truly be with others – being present and not keeping our phones in our hands and headphones in our ears. We have to create the right environment for communication to be fostered.

Science is continually showing us ways in which our bodies are connected to others. The work of Stephen Porges on the PolyVagal Theory that I mentioned in the chapter on curiosity has been taken and developed by others. Deb Dana, the author of 'The Rhythm of Regulation',[47] guides us to learn more about how we can regulate our nervous system. Using the work of Porges, she teaches simple strategies to help us understand the hierarchy of the nervous system, the effect of neuroception[48] on the body and the power of co-regulation. By learning about our nervous system, we can learn to identify the impact of trauma on our body. We can recognise when we become disconnected and when our parasympathetic nervous system gets stuck. If any of this piques your interest I would wholeheartedly recommend you read Deb Dana's book, which is my go-to learning resource on this subject.

The important thing to remember is that having a positive community around us enables us to share the joys of being in 'ventral vagal'. Ventral vagal is when we instinctively respond to cues of safety from our environment and from people around us. As I write these words, I am sitting on the deck of my sister's house in Santa Cruz. I feel safe here, surrounded by the redwood trees, with blue sky peeking through the branches. There is the sound of dripping water behind me as my brother-in-law finishes watering the plants. A hummingbird or two flit between the trees searching for sweetness to boost those incredibly fast wings. In humans, the cues of safety will be the easy look we get from people who want to connect with us, the warm smile on their lips, the sharing of a quick joke or two. Their skin will have colour and their face will be animated. Think of this compared to a blank or hard gaze with a pursed lip or straight mouth and tension in the skin that can warn us of danger ahead.

Community and our bodies

How does the feeling of community show up for us in our bodies? I am going to share an experience you may already be familiar with. Imagine walking into a party for a good friend. As you walk in you scan the room with a smile to try to connect with others you know, seeking out a smile returned freely. Community for me is often seen on faces and then experienced in our hearts. The joy of connection is reflected in our physical movements, such as moving towards others or reaching out for a hug or a kiss.

Our heart is an energetic battery and like any battery, it needs energy to keep it charged. It seeks to make connections with others. Our heart is where our compassion lies, including in our relationship with the world. Compassion is our desire to act in support of another. Compassion and empathy drive connections. Our hearts do not have a language centre, so when we feel drained emotionally, we use metaphors to share this, such as being 'out of sorts' or even 'heartsick'.

Our hands then develop that feeling of community. My hands connect me with you as I write my thoughts. My hands connect with others in the simplest of things; a caress or a handhold can convey volumes to another, without the need for words. Recently, I have been with my sister as she has been taking the next step in her post-cancer journey. As the consultant shared some very positive news, the first thing I wanted to do was to reach out and hug her. That hug was my way to share so much, including relief, joy, congratulations and more.

Spend a moment or two reflecting on how you have physically connected with another person today. If that is not an option for you, maybe spend a moment or two connecting with yourself with some supportive self-touch. Do you need a hug from yourself as a reminder that you are doing well, a small stroke of the skin on your hand as a comfort for the trials and tribulations you are dealing with in your life?

How do you or could you use physical touch or gesture to convey a thought of care to people in your community?

What difference does a focus on community make to how I lead?

In thinking about the people-helping professionals I have worked with, I have created a pen portrait for a very common type of leader or person who is often disconnected. I have called him 'David', in my table overleaf; you might remember him from the introduction. Here I show you how David's disconnection can be transformed by using *The Change Flywheel* model to 'support yourself'.

David recognises the power of community to help us when we get to a certain stage in our life and know that we need new learning. Having support can make that leap feel less daunting; none of us need ever do it alone. There is always someone who can support us in our decision-making. What we have to let go of is the need to do it all on our own. To build communities, some of the barriers have to come down.

Sometimes as leaders we find ourselves stuck in our comfort zones, where we tend to anticipate threat rather than connection. I am reminded of times meeting parents as a headteacher, when I would expect the worst rather than staying open and more neutral. Knowing how to soften our facial expressions and tone of voice in meeting these potentially challenging encounters can help ease the tension for everyone present.

The Change Flywheel

Original disconnected thought	New community thought	Result
Oh dear, another two hours wasted on that website. If someone tracked my internet history they would laugh: life after 50, living abroad, starting up your own business, how a dog can change your life – mmmm, maybe it was three hours, not two.	Wow, this morning has gone so fast. I have had so many productive conversations with my team and my boss. Time has flown by in a great way.	Focused, attentive and productive, David is keen to share his learning with his community.
It's not that I don't like my job. I just know there has to be something else. I'm only four years off early retirement – I could hang on until then.	I like my job but can also see that there is something else I would like to do. I always remember my first boss who said – start to plan to leave when everything is going well. That way you make the right decisions about the next stage in your life.	David recognises that no job is forever. In fact, the days of life-long jobs are rapidly passing and that's a good thing. David's strengths could be useful in any job, whether paid or unpaid. Recognising that the time to go is when you are in a good mental state, saves heartache, stress and possible burnout.
The pension people say I should work nine more years but there's no way I can wait that long.	I have been feeling a sense of 'what next?' I have engaged a coach to support me in gaining clarity. I know that community is key to whatever I do next.	David recognises that he doesn't have to make all the decisions on his own. Key people can help him – pension advisers, union reps, therapists and coaches.
But, I also know that I don't want to just hang up my hat. They say that 50 is the new 30, but Ibiza is not what I want. In fact, in my day it was Magaluf – now I'm really showing my age! Yes, seaside life has its attractions – now where was that last tab?	I have really enjoyed turning 50. It feels fresh and not just the start of a new decade. We are born, we die and the living is in between. No sense in harking back to the past ... what is piquing my interest right now? Might have a chat with Caroline from HR, she's always got a creative method or two to help make a decision.	David is bringing other elements of *The Change Flywheel* into play here. He is curious about what's next, motivating himself to try something new, engaging his community to support him to make that change.

People-helping professionals reading this now might be thinking: 'Well, Sam, my world is all about community.' Maybe your work is in a school community or a healthcare setting or a law firm. The people we work with absolutely provide us with support, encouragement and learning. However, a leader who relies too much on one community base can find themselves speaking and working in a silo. Being mindful about creating and engaging in different communities supports leaders in keeping the communities they lead fresh and growing.

Be courageous and assign time for creating and joining new communities. As with the example I gave about knitting, these communities can be in-person or online, in your local area, your country or worldwide.

I completed my own coach training while I was working as a headteacher. I had no desire to leave my work in full-time education but made the decision to do my coach training outside of an educational setting. I did that because I knew that there was much to learn from other professionals who came from different backgrounds. There were many positive ways of working that I knew could be brought into my world of education. Being coached and coaching others outside my sector, reminded me that the pressures I had working in my field were very similar to those of people-helping professionals in other fields. The notion that we are often on our own dissipated and I felt much more connected to leaders across all sectors.

To this day, I really enjoy working with clients from other professions. My own coaches have been people who have worked in a variety of industry sectors.

Building a wide range of communities helps us to build up a good set of secure bases. In his lifelong work as a psychologist and consultant, George Kohlriser[49] talks about secure bases as a *'person, place, goal or object that provides a sense of protection, gives a sense of comfort and offers a source of energy and exploration to explore, take risks and seek change'*.

When considered in the context of community, secure bases are people. I have had several secure bases that I could draw on for protection, comfort and energy in my work as a headteacher and now as a coach. These have included my eldest sisters, ex-colleagues and my husband.

Different communities support us in addressing our own cognitive biases, such as how we approach working with different ages or cultural backgrounds, or simply how we choose to tackle a project. Diversity is essential in all aspects of our work. Having a diverse community in our own workplace helps enhance creativity and learning about different cultural perspectives; it also improves the opportunity to reach a wider community. Having a diverse cultural community also brings in new knowledge about how things work and are organised, and is known to inject unique perspectives into decision-making.[50]

Building communities gives leaders a golden opportunity to work in multi-generational settings.[51] Learning to connect across generations from Gen Z to the baby boomers provides an ideal opportunity for learning. A multigenerational workforce is one in which the employees span different generations. There are now five generations existing simultaneously in the workforce (Gen Z, millennials, Gen X, baby boomers and some members of the silent generation still working into their late seventies and early eighties) – a first in modern history.

When you establish good connections across generations there are huge benefits. Learning and openness can undo damaging stereotypes and lead to growth for all. They decrease cognitive bias, increase knowledge and help us share wisdom. We can learn to adapt our communication style to meet the needs of each generation in respectful and understanding ways.

I recently came across a wonderful YouTube video by Joy France[52] who decided that she wanted to challenge herself at the age of 64. She embarked on a journey to 'grow old playfully', and in doing so helped others to find their voice by exploring creativity in all its forms. Focusing on similarities between generations rather than differences makes a wonderful leadership recipe for success. Her 'rap poetry battles' are a joy to listen to.

One of the simplest ways for a leader to develop a sense of community is to share food with others. At work, move away from your desk and go and eat with a colleague. At home, if you live with others – take time to eat with them. If you are living and working alone, make an effort to go to places where others congregate, such as cafes, restaurants or community centres. The simple act of eating with others, or eating alone with others around you, helps us stave off the hardship of loneliness. It also helps create a world where new communities can be formed, deeper connections can be made and new ideas can be born. And this shared understanding can help break down the many barriers that we all face in our daily lives.

CHANGE FLYWHEEL TAKEAWAYS

COMMUNITY – support yourself

- How do the communities you belong to help you maintain emotional well-being?

- How can you use the power of touch to support yourself or someone in your community today?

- What biases are preventing you from connecting with communities?

- What strategies can you deploy to grow a multigenerational working community?

How can developing community help me create my future self?

Stories are key to thriving communities. Those stories have taught us lessons about the world that we hold to be true; they shape our beliefs in both positive and negative ways. As this is a book about empowerment, we are going to use this section to identify positive stories that we already have about the world and who we are. We are also going to create positive future stories that will shape and support what we want to happen in the world.

Activity 1: Identify role models or significant teachers from your life whose attributes guide and support you.

Time needed: an hour.

Aim: to bring to the forefront of your mind positive role models and to make connections with who you are.

This is an exercise that I use when working with new leaders on my course, *Evolution*.

Think about the people with whom, or for whom, you have worked and who you consider to be great leaders or teachers.

Write down the names of those people you feel have brought out the best in you. Pick between three and four names. There is space over the page to write your list.

Next to each name, list the qualities, characteristics and attitudes that you believe make these people great leaders. Be sure to list qualities that are related to the whole person: mind, body and attitude to life.

The Change Flywheel

What similarities if any do you notice among these people?

As you contemplate these people, reflect on how some or all of these attributes are ones you aspire to have or already have yourself. How do you know? What impact do these attributes have on other people around you in your community?

....
....
....
....
....
....
....
....
....
....
....
....
....
....
....
....
....
....
....
....
....
....
....
....
....

Activity 2: Identify your own personal or professional council of elders.

Time needed: work on this over one day.

Aim: to identify core values that you admire in others and might want to develop for yourself.

I have taken this activity from the work of Sharon Blackie and the *Hagitude*[53] community, and have then combined it with recognised works on archetypes.

If you had your own 'council of elders', who would you choose to guide you in your life? Who would you put on the council and why? Now unlike the previous activity, these people could be real or imagined. To support you in creating your council, I have listed below different archetypes that you might draw from.

What is an archetype?

Archetypes are universal, inborn models of people, behaviours, and personalities that play a role in influencing human behaviour. Swiss psychiatrist Carl Jung suggested that these archetypes were archaic forms of innate human knowledge passed down from our ancestors.

Common archetypes

Mother or caregiver	Empath
Creator	Rebel
Explorer	Sage
Joker	Mentor
Magician	

There are many more if you care to research archetypes.

The Change Flywheel

To make this more challenging, I would like you to keep your council of elders to a council of nine, drawing on my favourite fantasy series the Lord of the Rings. Who are they and what roles do they provide for you?

The aim of this is for you to draw on their experience when you need it.

How do you do that? It's very simple. You ask yourself: what would [name of elder] say in response to a particular question? Then see if you can let their perspective support your decision-making. Even if you are not with them physically, their wisdom will still support you in building your communities.

....
....
....
....
....
....
....
....
....
....
....
....
....
....
....
....
....
....
....
....

INTERVIEW WITH HEATHER WARING

Heather Waring works with women who feel they have lost themselves on life's path. They have reached a crossroads or a stile on the track and need a trusted guide by their side. Heather is that woman. Her clients often face burnout as they tend to put themselves last before work and family. She too experienced burnout and now uses her journey back to wellness to support others. She helps them rediscover and reconnect with their true selves and then together they reignite that spark and essence.

Introduction

'Happiness is not a destination but a way of life.'

The sign on the wall over Heather's shoulder perfectly set the scene for this interview.

Heather was on the path to burnout long before she made any changes to better her life. She knew for a long time that she had hit rock bottom and should have been changing her lifestyle. She believes that in the society we currently live in we are biologically programmed as women, brought up and culturally conditioned to be there for everyone else and to put others first.

'Generally, many women find themselves putting themselves last and jumping in and helping everyone else.'

We fear that looking after ourselves means letting others down. With experience, however, I know that when you look after yourself through consistent daily self-care practices then you are better placed and better resourced to look after others.

I met Heather in 2018 when I had just embarked on my business path as a Leadership Energy coach. We shared membership in a national networking group of women and I was drawn to her energy which simply oozes out of her pores.

Heather's recent blog post was about modern daily morning rituals. Her routines change depending on her moods, what is going on in her life and the seasons.

'Routines bookend your day.'

Heather's energy is infectious. She adeptly draws you into her world and without knowing it you are soon walking by her side.

Five questions about your work and approach to life

Curiosity

In the words of Stephen Hawking: *'Remember to look up at the stars and not down at your feet. Try to make sense of what you see and wonder about what makes the universe exist. Be **curious**. And however difficult life may seem, there is always something you can do and succeed at.'*

How do you keep your curiosity alive in the work that you do today?

'I love that element of curiosity. You know, where's that? What's that? Let's go and find out.'

This question clearly resonated with Heather. One of her hashtags is: #becuriousonfoot. This links perfectly with the quote on her wall. With her profound love of walking, she nurtures her curiosity when she is out and about in the world in a rural or urban setting. Heather reminded me that even on a regular daily walk, new interests can appear: the way the light falls or the quality of the colours – or maybe even spotting a little alleyway that your eyes have never picked up before.

Heather demonstrated as she was talking how important looking up, physically, is for her. The sky, buildings or tree canopies take her into a different world and help her see life in new ways. The sights in her world inspire new thinking.

Mentally 'looking up' is 'not about having a closed mind. It's about keeping an open mind. *'It's about questioning, not necessarily taking things for granted. It's not necessarily taking what somebody says as being the absolute truth.'*

Those last few words led Heather into talking about her passion for alternative healthcare. She isn't suggesting that traditional medicines are not important, but in her mind, they are not the be-all and end-all.

She truly believes that if she had only followed the traditional medicine route when she was in the depths of burnout, she would have taken all the blame onto her own shoulders. Many of the tests that were done at the time came back positive but the signs of burnout were not pieced together. However, we all know that we cannot be experts in all things and this also applies to our overworked GPs; there is a danger in putting our health in the hands of people who have only done general practitioner training. It is practically not possible for GPs to train in everything. Heather was very curious and discovered alternative therapies that supported her.

More recently, she has managed to overcome a condition she has had since her twenties – fidgety legs. She has sought advice from many professionals within both the traditional and natural health services. By giving up gluten she believes it has helped her condition. Her curiosity has led her to sort out a lot of her health issues.

Heather's love of alternative ways of thinking has helped shape her life in very positive ways. She is a great believer in numerology and has worked with a numerologist for eight years. She is comfortable with the idea that in life we experience years of growth and years of consolidation. From a numerological perspective, she is now living in Year 9 which is a year of consolidation – an opportunity to look back at all the previous years and prepare to go into the next one; this will take her back to year one, a year of expansion. As Heather was talking, I could see how this system fitted into other development cycles that I knew. We all go through periods of growth and consolidation.

Alternative therapies and beliefs support the work that she does with her own clients, and she continuously uses walking as a tool to get to the heart of an issue.

Courage

It takes courage to be a leader. Thinking about the key leaders in your life, how did their courage support you to be more courageous in your life?

We often look to big acts of courage, but there are many stories of people who have taken courageous actions in smaller ways. Courage also shows up in our everyday life, for example in dealing with a negative health diagnosis.

Heather related the experience of a very close friend of hers whom she had met through work many years ago. Her friend had retired and set up a catering business. Last year, when celebrating their birthdays, her friend told her that she had discovered some unidentified lumps that were being investigated. Within a month, she had been diagnosed with stage three ovarian cancer. One day, after the diagnosis, she asked Heather for support with her decision to not take any treatment for the cancer. The decision was made in a way that was right for her. This woman was a life-loving person. Heather called her a leader not just for the work she did but more for the way she led in her groups of friends.

There was always an element of surprise whenever Heather met this particular friend. '*She had a way of making you feel really special,*' Heather explained.

The decision to not have treatment inspired Heather to be courageous for her friend on the day of her funeral and was also a reminder to continue to be courageous in her own life.

Another expression of courage for Heather is saying sorry and admitting weakness. Being humble and showing humility is, to her, a marker of a courageous person.

As Heather was growing up, there were several leaders she knew who took responsibility for their actions. In her first job in London, she worked with a grassroots charity with a small team. At the start of her time there, there was a mix-up with some information that had a large impact on the growing team. Some of this mix-up was due to the team not being fully technically aware of how to use the IT they had available to them.

Holding up her hands, Heather's boss accepted responsibility for the mix-up, didn't try to push the blame onto others and worked through the mistake. As Heather remarked, this woman *'taught me a lot about her management style, how to work with others; she definitely taught me about how to own our mistakes.'*

'Persistence and fairness are part of what makes a great leader.'

At the start of her coaching career, Heather worked with a coach–mentor. She realised quite quickly that the coaching model that this person was promoting was the antithesis of how Heather had been trained. She had learned that coaches were facilitators of the client's agenda. Heather pushed back against tying people into programmes that they didn't need and periods of time that clearly wouldn't work for them. The aim of the coaching programmes that were being promoted to her was: 1) to make a lot of money, and 2) to skew the work–life balance much more to work than to other aspects of her life. Having previously been singed by burnout, Heather knew that she needed to stay true to the courage of her convictions and walk her own path. Heather remarked that this was a life-long challenge for many people: being able to say *'No sorry, I don't agree with this'* and *'I'm not going to do that'*.

I asked Heather if one of her early parenting figures had helped shape this way of being. She responded that, on the contrary, her parents had lived their lives doing what was expected of them. Their way of living did have an impact on Heather, as well as growing up amid the troubles in Northern Ireland.

When you are living in a divided country, and city, it has a huge impact on your life. Rather than just accepting life as it was, Heather wanted to understand why this was happening. She did a huge amount of reading and learning, and made the brave decision that she did not want to continue living in this divided way, moving first to Scotland and then later to London.

Heather could see how easy it was to get *'entrenched in one view or another'* and continued to talk about not wanting to be *'pigeon-holed in certain things'*. As she was talking, I had an image of a bird not wanting to have its wings clipped.

Heather is a woman who wants to shake up society's views about what people can and cannot do at certain ages. She related a recent incident during a health assessment when a nurse asked her for a list of medications that she was taking. When she said she wasn't taking any, the nurse was clearly shaken, having never encountered a woman in her early sixties who was not taking pills for something. The conversation continued, resulting in the nurse – a woman in her early fifties – saying it was too late for her to have any personal development. Rather than letting this pass, Heather gently remonstrated with her in a *'Heather way'*, something which left the nurse reconsidering her self-image. It is so easy for others to put us in boxes, and it is up to us to ensure that we don't box ourselves in.

Creativity

**In the words of the late great Sir Ken Robinson*: 'I believe this passionately that we don't grow into creativity; we grow out of it or rather we get educated out of it.'*

What advice would you give schools to help children develop their creative thinking?

'I suppose in our ideal world, we let go of the curriculum.'

Heather went on to share what that would mean.

'It would allow teachers to bring their creativity, which they would have to re-learn.'

Many of us, including Heather, were brought up with the notion that to be creative you had to be good at an arts-based subject such as music or painting. In her re-learning, Heather realises that we are all creative and all can be creative. For teachers, their own creativity would be unleashed in their choice to deliver a style of learning that would really meet the needs of the children they are working with.

The teacher's job would be to facilitate the learning of the children, which would include any creative thinking.

Leading on from this idea, Heather talked about getting rid of the tick boxes that plague teachers, the constant measuring of test results to get you from here to there.

There would have to be some education for parents too so they can also learn to identify which institution might be right for their child rather than relying on the narrow parameters of Ofsted. She also talked about the need for parents to let their children live their own life, rather than the one they wished they could have lived as a child.

Heather gave the wonderful example of her nephew who has successfully built a landscaping and building firm from scratch. At school, he was told that he was not good enough and didn't seem to fit in. He was made to feel like someone with no hope just because his skills didn't fit the skill set of what the school was measuring.

The damage done to this one young man has been replicated across the country. With support, however, he was able to overcome the labelling that plagued him.

Schools must see children for who they are and Heather supports the premise that all teachers should have coach training as a matter of good practice.

We also agreed that teachers must get more comfortable in saying 'I *don't know*' and in supporting the children to find out for themselves.

Community

For many years, I have had a postcard above my desk outlining '44 ways to build community'. What communities do you lead or have you led in the past, and what helped them grow?

Heather started talking about the biggest community she has helped build over the past three years – her Facebook community of 8,200 global women. She gathered 1000 women in its first month and it is still growing now. She has women in Europe, North America, Australia and New Zealand, India, Singapore and the Philippines. I am sure there are, by now, many more countries and continents involved. What helped this community grow was word of mouth: women shared with other women.

Heather launched the community in November 2019, and in March 2020 the world went into lockdown in response to the Covid 19 outbreak. Women used the group as a way of connecting with other women they couldn't connect with in person. Photographs were used as inspiration and hope for many. One person's winter was another person's summer. The sunshine photos and snowy scenes lifted the spirits of those unable to move very far away from their homes.

Genuine relationships have been formed and many of these women have gone on to meet up in person. These Facebook posts helped motivate the lonely. None of us need to be alone – a walking partner might be found just around the corner.

In supporting this group to feel safe, some rules were quickly put into place when a few took advantage and started selling inappropriate products or services. With clear boundaries in place, the trust then grows.

Heather enjoys working online and in person and has always had private Facebook groups for her clients to experience what it is like working with her. Trust builds safety and that builds connection. In the safe space she creates, she can see people being honest about what they need. A short helpful comment may be all someone needs to kickstart them on the road to a new life.

Heather has regularly led groups to walk sections of the Camino de Santiago, in Northern Spain. Each group has a WhatsApp group to help them get to know each other. These small groups of ten or so women build a sense of community even before they set foot on the pilgrim's way.

So much of Heather's work is interwoven like a perfect spider's web.

Change

Change is the only constant in our lives or so the saying goes. How do you keep harmony in your life and your work?

Heather was quite emphatic about this: 'It comes back to curiosity. What brings me harmony in my life is growing, *looking ahead and not settling.*' This curiosity helps Heather look for potential new growth in her life.

Knowing herself helps and each year she uncovers a bit more about who she is and what makes her tick. Recently, Heather did some work on her DNA, learning more about the impact of her DNA on her biology. She recognises that she absolutely needs sunshine and so now has regular breaks away to get that sunshine fix. Sometimes the break will be just to another space to work for the day or a longer time abroad. It is in these quiet times that Heather can get perspective on her work and life, and to make the minor adjustments she needs for greater harmony.

Heather is blessed with a partner who has similar needs and who is happy for her to go off on her own. But harmony is also achieved with regular partner time, enjoying the good things in life. She achieves a sense of balance and harmony that suits both of them. They clearly prioritise restoration in their lives.

How does Heather embody my *Change Flywheel* coaching model?

Heather is constantly curious about her life and body. Searching for possible guidance from a wide network, she is not content with the status quo. That enquiring mind takes her into courageous places, standing up for women whose voices are not heard by others. Heather is always open to learning and encourages others to re-create the version of themselves that has been shaped by those who do not have their best interests at heart. Heather's warmth and love for others have led her to not only support but lift others up through the art of walking. She is a woman who – one step at a time – walks change into her life and the lives of others.

HEATHER'S TAKEAWAYS

Curiosity: It's about questioning, not necessarily taking things for granted. Thinking about your work right now, what might you be taking for granted?

Courage: Small or big acts of courage? List five small acts of courage you have achieved over the past five months. What key strengths did you use to be courageous?

Creativity: When was the last time you said 'I don't know' and then went on to be creative in finding out?

Community: When have your boundaries been breached in a community you have led? What could you do to repair the damage?

Change: Time alone and time with others: spend a minute reflecting on the balance you have in your life between these two things.

INTERVIEW WITH RICHARD LAYZELL

Richard is an award-winning artist, performer, teacher, writer, creative ecologist and course director at Skyros Holidays. His creative project 'The Naming' took him to five continents. He is a lecturer with the University of Arts London and the author of 'Enhanced Performance', 'Cream Pages' and 'The Naming'.

Introduction:

I worked with Richard as a young teacher at my first school.

Richard was commissioned to work as a performance artist with schools in the late eighties and early nineties. I had the pleasure of working with him on two separate occasions. Those were the days when we could spend a whole term on an extended art project. The work revolved around an art installation that my class built that was exhibited in a gallery in Southwark. We built the House of Nations out of rubbish.

Richard's off-the-wall work with me had a huge impact on my relationship with creativity and emboldened me to be more courageous in my work. This is why I was keen to interview him and hear more about his current work.

The Change Flywheel

Five questions about your work and approach to life

Curiosity

In the words of Stephen Hawking: *'Remember to look up at the stars and not down at your feet. Try to make sense of what you see and wonder about what makes the universe exist. Be **curious**. And however difficult life may seem, there is always something you can do and succeed at.'*

How do you keep your curiosity alive in the work that you do today?

'For me, it is quite connected to when you train as an artist – even in the first year of your study, your eyes are kind of opened and everything shifts and it doesn't really go back.'

Curiosity for Richard was intrinsically connected with his early training. From the moment he started his artistic studies he started to see the world in a very different way. He has stayed visually curious about the world since then.

At the time of the interview, he was in a period of reflection, given it took place in the middle of the second lockdown.

He was completing a piece of work linked to some Arts Council funding which had been a challenge to secure. At the time he had started the work, everyone else was having to stay inside. Due to the relevance of his work to nature, he was able to work outside.

As there were no social distancing issues he was free to be curious about the most mundane of things, including the unexplored corners of car parks. In his explorations, Richard discovered: *'areas of wilderness that are genuinely flourishing in car park spaces that people have stopped using. This was a discovery that I hadn't expected to find and I guess curiosity leads to more.'*

Richard has particular practices that he uses to nourish his curiosity, many stemming from his childhood when he loved being outside.

In the first lockdown, he would do the same walk early every day. Each day he would see something different and make notes in his journal. These early morning walks became a way of life for Richard.

As another way to see things differently, he has also developed fictional collaborators and voices, like characters in a novel. He discusses ideas with them regularly, through the written word. It's a way of being forced to see things differently. One of these is Kino Paxton, who is listed as a collaborator on his website and social media profile.

His curiosity had also been piqued by my reaching out to interview him. He found himself revisiting a pile of 35mm slides and remembering the work he had done on a previous project. This remembering led him to think about a possible new idea for a book. He'd thought this previous project was done and dusted but now, at this new point in his life, he saw he might be able to make something vibrant and interesting from it.

Courage

It takes courage to be a leader. Thinking about the key leaders in your life – how did their courage support you to be courageous in your life?

Richard was born in Acton and brought up in Greenford in what he called a lower middle-class neighbourhood. His parents struggled with finances and, he told me later, their own relationship. Unusually, his primary school was just for boys. He had two male teachers whom he could trust. Each supported him to make school a safe place, in contrast to the chaotic nature of his home. They provided clear boundaries for him and, as leaders, they modelled clarity and discipline with kindness.

After passing the 11 Plus, he went on to the local boys' grammar school. The competitive and uncaring culture did not meet his needs and, as a sensitive teen, his self-esteem collapsed. Exacerbated by burgeoning adolescence and more turbulence at home, Richard found solace in the art room and outdoors – through the Duke of Edinburgh's Award Scheme and his involvement with the air cadets.

There was one teacher who was very kind to Richard, an alternative Liverpudlian English teacher who liked his writing. He saw something in him that others did not. The encouragement he got from this teacher supported his desire to go to art school. Richard went on to study on a Foundation Art and Design course at Ealing School of Art where he was surrounded by young teachers who gave him encouragement and confidence. Each of them acknowledged the artist in him. They encouraged him to apply to the Slade School of Art, where he studied for the next five years.

What this piece tells me about Richard is how these significant teachers in his life would have shaped the teacher he went on to become.

Richard then went on to tell me about a professional relationship he had had with someone who had significantly influenced his working life. He had met this person whilst teaching on the island of Skyros. Strangely, he had the same name, age and birth sign. With these auspicious connections, he challenged Richard and invited him to come and work at his company. With courage Richard agreed, on the terms that he would come as an artist-in-residence, setting his own salary and an initial length of service of three months. Richard worked closely with the other Richard for five years and eventually had a budget of half a million pounds and the title of *Visionaire*.

This leader wanted the absolute best for his company. He gave Richard space and time to work with his colleagues, without micromanaging him. That space allowed the team to think in a creative way. In doing so, the company achieved great things.

As Richard reflected on the leaders in his life, he recognised that he had learned some key traits from them. He discovered a facility for running workshops which led to him being part of the newly formed Skyros Community in his early thirties. For the past thirty years, he has been one of the course directors of Skyros, heading up the teacher team.

As a director, he is comfortable being himself: *'someone who isn't particularly demonstrative, isn't particularly strict but has an overview where people feel safe, respected and supported... people have a lot of freedom and feel safe to be experimenting, to be playful, take risks and be vulnerable.'*

As we finished talking about courage, Richard wanted to add this:

'I think that there is a lot of misunderstanding about courage. I think people are more courageous than they realise. For some, they think I'm being courageous standing up in front of people as a solo performer. But for me, that is easy – challenging but not

impossible. It is not a huge courageous risk. They might tell me that they could not possibly do what I do. But that doesn't mean that they are not courageous. They are demonstrating courage in all kinds of places. Just think of all the people in the NHS at the moment. They have no choice about being courageous.'

We finished this discussion on courage by talking about staff in public sector jobs who showed up every day during the pandemic, supporting all of us and keeping our society going whilst many of us hid indoors. Thank you NHS, teachers, transport workers, shopkeepers, police, fire and more – for your duty, sense of vocation and courage.

Creativity

In the words of the late great Sir Ken Robinson: *'I believe this passionately – that we don't grow into creativity; we grow out of it or rather we get educated out of it.'*

What advice would you give schools to help children develop their creative thinking?

Richard has a daughter at primary school who does not think she can draw. He knows that she got this lack of creative confidence from a society that consistently judges creativity against very small parameters. The narrow way in which the arts are taught in schools right now does concern him.

'Schools tell us we cannot sing, dance, draw. If children have all of these messages by the time they are eleven it is hard to re-engage with the process as an adult.'

His advice would be that schools specifically teach creativity through a creative thinking model. He thinks that if we continue in the way we have been teaching them we will continue to stifle creative development for all our children. I would have to agree with Richard here. The narrow curriculum on offer to children in the UK does not allow them space to be creative. The constant focus on basic skills hampers progress across all aspects of their lives. The children who are boosted and tutored to do well in their SATs in primary school are taken out of PE, art, music and any other lesson where they could make connections with learning.

In Richard's mind, creative learning supports so much of who we are and, in particular, our wellbeing. What reinvigorated it for him was outdoor learning as well as the space that a particular teacher gave him to make connections.

The challenge is for schools – but most importantly for the government via the Department for Education – to recognise and champion creativity. It would mean current school leaders being open to finding out what creativity means for them personally before embedding new practices and thinking in their own schools.

Community

For many years, I have had a postcard above my desk outlining '44 ways to build community'. What communities do you lead or have you led in the past, and what helped them grow?

It became apparent during this interview that Richard thrives on being involved with creative communities. After his degree, in his early artist days, he worked on a radical Open University course called 'Art and Environment', which had a legendary reputation for being very creative and anarchic. He took this exploratory curriculum to the island of Skyros when he began working there.

Richard was very keen to explain how simple regular structures helped the communities he worked in to grow and thrive. He outlined how the people in the Skyros community work together to enable everyone to feel part of the experience, even if they are only there for one or two weeks. They gather together at the beginning of the week and introduce themselves to each other – participants, teachers and tutors. This collective group then meets several times a day during the week or fortnight.

'Every day, the group meets over breakfast. This is called 'demos', from this Greek word that means commune, led by one person and we have a structure to go through announcements, appreciations, announcements from teachers. A bit like an assembly.

Following this they then have workgroups when people help in the community – sweeping, chopping vegetables, etc., and many other group structures, like 'ekos' groups where people meet in groups of 8 for an hour – a confidential space where everyone is seen as equal. This therapeutic group runs in the form of a circle with each person given three minutes to speak to the rest of the group.

They also assign co-listeners where you can meet for half an hour with one person. Half an hour together, one person speaks for five minutes, the other person listens. The person who is listening reports back what they heard them say. There is no interrupting. It is listening and sharing and then you swap. They hear back what they have said from partners.'

As the community is based in a remote part of the island, the participants gather together most evenings to attend talks, workshops and expressive activities.

All of these structures build a strong community, held by Richard or his co-director. He shared with me that he has learned a huge amount about how to build a community from these structures. They provide the framework that holds a community together.

Change

Change is the only constant in our lives – or so the saying goes. How do you keep harmony in your life or in your work?

'I think it is partly about having some control and some boundaries.'

Richard was very clear here. He understood that having boundaries in life is what kept his life harmonious. His early childhood wasn't like that as he was a sickly child. At one point he wasn't even sure he was going to make it. He had acute lung problems, collapsed lungs and bronchitis. For a period of time, he was genuinely fighting to stay alive. He remembers this as a frightening experience, especially coupled with his parents being on the verge of splitting up. He felt that life was unstable.

Creating stability helped him to deal with the chaos. He had to develop some strength to take care of himself. He nurtured tenacity and worked hard on self-development.

As a performance artist, he learned to project his voice. The tenets of Tai Chi, yoga and regular meditation have really supported him to keep harmony in his life.

As we reached the end of the interview, Richard commented on how useful these structures were, particularly in the first lockdown. When a huge amount of change whirls around us, he feels they keep us grounded and productive.

How does Richard embody my *Change Flywheel* coaching model?

Richard keeps that curious mindset and strives continually to know himself. He shows courage in pushing the boundaries of his artistic experience and stepping out of his known world into the unknown. He enriches himself through creative endeavour on a daily basis. He supports and is supported by wide-ranging communities, from his own family to the creative community on the island of Skyros. His acceptance of change allows all of the future potential Richard to come to fruition. Richard shared that he is sometimes surprised by his own energy. He laughed as he talked about the need to explore more and more. He thrives on the connection between energy and flow; for him, it is ultimately life-affirming:

'The relationship between energy and flow is very close and I get so thrilled by it at times, I'm shocked.'

RICHARD'S TAKEAWAYS

Curiosity: *'It is so liberating to be curious about mundane things.'* What mundane things need some of your curiosity right now?

Courage: *'I am comfortable being myself – someone who isn't particularly demonstrative, isn't particularly strict but has a kind of overview where people feel safe and respected and supported.'* Do people feel safe and supported by you? If not, what could you change?

Creativity: What would you put into a creativity curriculum?

Community: *'I organised meetings like events – they were fun, they were orchestrated, they were like a production.'* How could you take this idea into the communities you lead?

Change: Energy + flow = life-affirming. What equation would you write for your life?

CHANGE

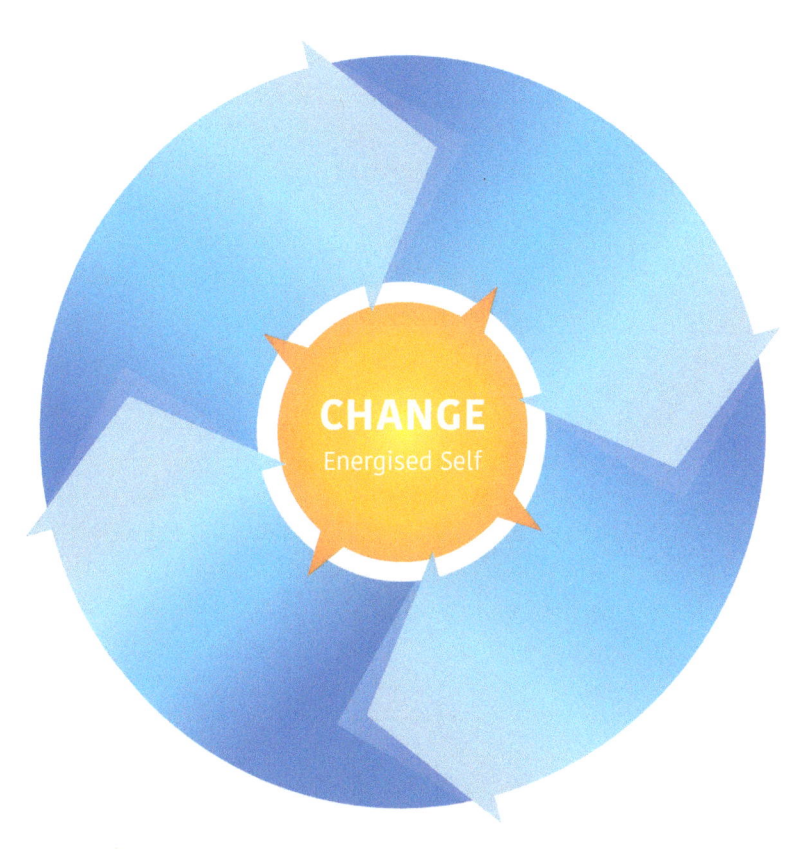

CHANGE
Energised Self

'The measure of intelligence is the ability to change.'

Albert Einstein

Change is an act or process through which something becomes different. It is transformation.

Transformation is what naturally occurs when you focus on the four tenets of *The Change Flywheel*. In being curious and finding out more about yourself, being courageous and motivating yourself, being creative and enriching yourself and using your community to support yourself, your energised self will emerge. It's a process about transformation for the better. *The Change Flywheel* supports you in connecting with yourselves, creating more energy and in doing so, putting you in a better place to connect with others.

And the outcome of this transformation? Not only does it reduce the overwhelm, disconnect and lack of confidence often faced by people-helping professionals, but it also improves relationships leading to a sense of greater harmony in our lives.

As you have been reading and undertaking the activities in this book, you may have gained useful insights about yourself. Some of these may have already enabled you to implement strategies to combat the negative effects of overwhelm. You may have also had some realisations but without finding a way forward – yet.

This chapter is intended to add to the momentum you need to make long-lasting changes in your life that both energise you and create more harmony.

Our understanding of change is essential to *The Change Flywheel*. The ancient Greek philosopher Heraclitus[54] is reputed to have said, '*Change is the only constant*' or as Seneca[55] put it, '*We both do and do not step twice into the same* river. Because, you see, the name of the river stays the same, but the water keeps flowing'.

In this constantly changing world that we live in, embracing change is necessary to save us from getting overwhelmed by the twists and turns of that river. To embrace change we need to build our capacity and our ability to adapt.

Instead of ancient Greek philosophy, let's turn to fairy tales to help us focus on change. In the story of Goldilocks, a young girl enters the house of the three bears. The porridge that she pilfers, the chairs that she breaks and the beds that she sleeps in are either too hot/cold, too large/small or too hard/soft, but she ends up finding the ones that are just right.

Taking that notion of 'just right' and applying it to change in relation to energy, we could ask ourselves – how does too much change, too little change or just the right amount of change affect the body, mind and our relationship with others?

That last row – just right – is *The Change Flywheel* in action. This is where we know ourselves, know how to motivate ourselves, have good strategies in place to enrich ourselves and are fully supported by our community. Here, we have sufficient energy to use for all aspects of our life.

To get to the 'just right' stage, I have found in my work that we need to consistently spend time with the 3 Rs – Resilience, Resourcing through rest and Regulation.

Change	Too much	Too little	Just right
Possible impact on our bodies	Racing heart, shallow breathing, feeling off balance, tight muscles, headaches, dizziness, churning gut, heartburn, sweating, disrupted sleep	Lethargy, oversleeping, inertia, sighing, feeling cold, gastro-intestinal problems	Energised, centred, rested, calm, steady and balanced breathing, happy, open
Possible impact on our mind	Anxious thoughts, constant list-building, lack of focus, multi-tasking, procrastination, interrupted work	Daydreaming, boredom, depression, rumination, guilt, lack of self-worth, sadness	Motivation, focus, flow, curious mindset
Possible impact on our relationship with others	Irritated, snappy, not present, unavailable and unsupportive, focused on own tasks not those of others	Dependent, distant, defensive, discord, co-dependent relationships	Connected, enthusiastic, empowered, engaged, enhanced morale and sense of fun, passionate, joyful, compassionate
Resulting feelings and experiences	Overwhelmed, lacking confidence, chaos	Disconnected, lacking confidence, constriction	Balance, coherence, all areas of life in harmony

Why does change matter to us as humans?

Let's start with resilience and the work of Carole Pemberton in her book Resilience.[56] She espouses that resilience is *'The capacity to remain flexible in our thoughts, feelings and behaviours when faced by a life disruption, or extended period of pressure, so that we emerge from difficulty stronger, wiser and more able.'*

Unlike the dictionary definition, this quote is not about bouncing back, taking hard knocks or being buoyant.

The keywords in Carole's definition are 'capacity' and 'flexible', and implicitly, adaptability and learning.

Taking those words, I continued with my learning and trained with Jenny Campbell and the Resilience Dynamic® team in 2017. This research shapes all my work with every client and team. It has proved to be an excellent tool that I use daily to take a close look at my own resilience levels.

Jenny's definition of resilience is *'our ability to adapt, it is our capacity for change'*. Her research started in 2007 and has been developed, refined and published in her book The Resilience Dynamic®.[57] This is the definition I use all the time and encourage you to also take it on.

For many people-helping professionals, the capacity for change is hard to build. Adaptability is even harder to come by when working with people who rely on you to do so much.

We build that capacity by reminding ourselves that, like a plant, we need the right conditions to grow. We are a part of nature, not apart from it. For humans, those right conditions are good sleep, good thinking time, good quality food and good movement. We also need time to connect with others.

The quickest way out of the stressful and depressed states of body and mind listed in the table above is to focus on sleeping, thinking, eating and moving. Dr Ranjan Chatterjee used similar words in his book The 4 Pillar Plan.[58]

A little mnemonic to remind you of these words was shared with the Resilience Dynamic® community by Anne Archer.[59] You take the first letter of each of these words – sleep, think, eat, move – and get the word STEM, to remember that, just like plants, we also need the right conditions to grow and thrive. We also need connections. From what biologists are finding out about plants, they too need the connections of other plants around them. If in doubt about this, I encourage you to read about the 'wood wide web'.[60]

I find that many of my people-helping clients find themselves getting stuck in the 'just coping' region of their resilience. The resilience dynamic framework classifies these as 'chronic copers'. It can be very hard for them to take any time out to address their needs for sleeping, thinking, eating and moving as this often makes them feel guilty – guilty that they are not thinking of the team. Remember that old adage, there is no I in the word team? Well, that has gone a long way in persuading caring professionals to always put themselves last. Their oxygen tank is already empty by the time they put their mask on. By that time, they are suffering the effects of either too much or too little change in their minds and bodies.

If you were to consider these four words – sleep, think, eat, move – which do you think would most benefit from five minutes of thought to boost your resilience?

Improved energy is the focus of *The Change Flywheel*, so energy management is one of the quickest ways to boost our resilience.

The Change Flywheel

A long-lasting way to boost energy is by developing the necessary knowledge and habits to enable rest.

Rest sits in the 'think' quadrant of STEM. Rest is essential to counteracting the overwork that many of us experience. It is the area of STEM that most professionals find hardest to cultivate. Why is that? Well, those old chestnuts come up again – fear, guilt, judgement, inadequacy. These are the limiting beliefs and negative emotions that whisper toxic nothings in our ears:

- I'll rest when the last spreadsheet is finished, no one likes a quitter
- This is the way we do things here, 7 a.m. to 8 p.m. It's just the way it is
- I need my emails on my phone, what if someone needs me?
- I can only rely on myself to get this job done
- If I don't do this now, I'll only have to do it later on
- No one in my team can get this job done better than me
- It's my name on the door, wall, website, letterhead etc.
- If I don't show them I can do this they won't believe in me as a leader
- If I leave to do my exercise class, they might think I am lazy

The phrasing might not be the same as above, but the thoughts will be similar. I've had many of these toxic phrases play out in my mind during my time as a leader in schools and I often hear similar comments from my clients.

The perception that rest equals laziness is huge. In a culture that sees productivity as king, we hold those who work long hours in high esteem, even though long hours have been proven to lower productivity. A shift is needed to recognise that the better leaders are the ones who know themselves, motivate themselves, enrich themselves and support themselves. They are more energised and focused leaders, able to show up when they work and when they rest.

As the entrepreneur Daniel Abrahams says, '*In 20 years from now, the only people who will remember you worked late will be your kids*' (or pets if you have them).

So how do you rest and what does rest actually mean?

Rather than a definition, these words might offer you an indication of rest: to relax, have leisure time, be silent, at ease, free to pause and decompress. One favourite idea of mine is that rest equals restoration. When we rest we are restoring and resetting positive energy, in contrast to the negative energy that can sap our focus and attention.

In his wonderful book 'Do Pause', Robert Poynton[61] outlines various ways in which we can learn to let go and put a pause into our day. We can often feel a bit like Sisyphus,[62] constantly pushing that rock up the hill, only for it to roll back down again. What if Sisyphus just left the rock at the bottom of the hill, sat with his back against it and paused for a while? What if he took in his surroundings – the hills, the sky, the warmth on his back? In giving up and letting go, he might just have found some enjoyment in other aspects of his life.

I have taken the word pause into my motto – pause, ponder, percolate. In these micro-moments that I put in between appointments and other parts of my day, I tune into my inner world and see what needs tending to. In these mini check-ins, I can also feel if it is time to let something go, rather than constantly pushing it uphill.

In her TED talk Saundra Dalton Smith[63] talks about the seven types of rest which I have used extensively in my work with teams and individuals. I also use them for myself. The seven types of rest are an excellent way to increase energy. The canny person will find ways to combine different types of rest. A great example of physical rest is jogging, which also covers sensory rest by taking you away from a screen. It covers mental rest too by giving you time to think, and spiritual rest by allowing you to expand your vision beyond your office. If you are in a running club, it also provides you with social rest, as you run with your group.

My favourite rest type is creative rest, where I engage my hands in making. It ticks many of the rest-type boxes for me: sensory rest as I enjoy the feel of different types of yarn or fabric, social rest as I craft with friends, and spiritual rest as I see the unfolding beneath my fingers. I find this truly restorative.

People-helping professionals often need sensory rest. Being 'on' all the time can wear you out; the laptop glare, mobile notifications, and constant online meetings can all sap your energy. Quick and quiet practices such as a screen break can refresh you in an instant.

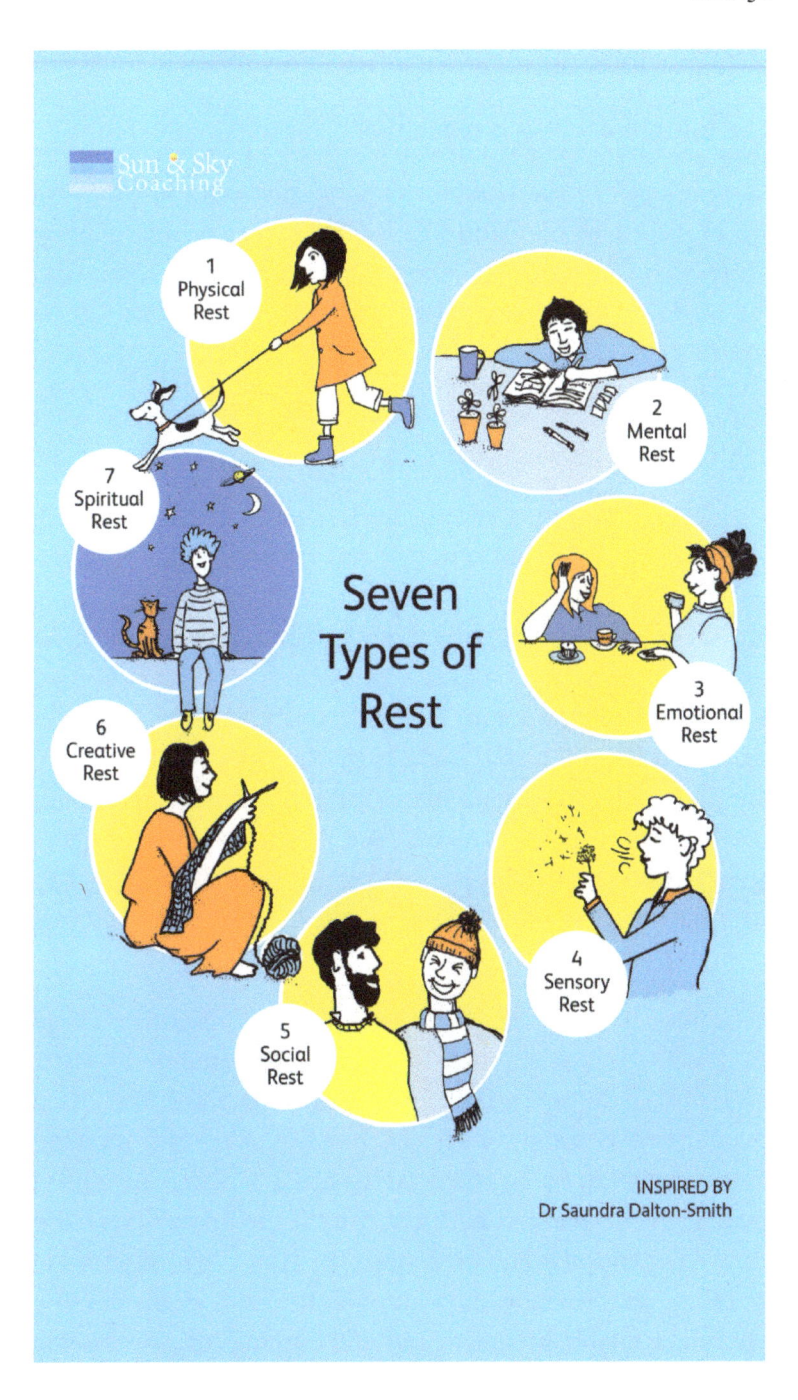

Change

Seven Types of Rest

1. Physical Rest
2. Mental Rest
3. Emotional Rest
4. Sensory Rest
5. Social Rest
6. Creative Rest
7. Spiritual Rest

Sun & Sky Coaching

INSPIRED BY
Dr Saundra Dalton-Smith

The Change Flywheel

Where does change sit in my body?

The third of my 3 Rs is regulation.

Linking back to the Goldilocks table, just right is when we are in a state of regulation. It is a state that people-helping professionals might not experience enough in their day: the state of ventral vagal that I discussed in the chapter on community.

These mini scenarios might help you better understand what ventral vagal might feel like for people-helping professionals.

Head Teacher You're standing at the gate in the morning on a cold winter's day, greeting the children as they come into school. You notice the way the parents have taken time to wrap up their children against the cold, the new shoes, or first-time tied laces, the squirmy puppy carried gently and firmly under the arm with the proud owners by the side, ready to share the joys and tribulations of puppy rearing with you. Here you feel the regular beat of your heart, your cold fingers inside your gloves, and see the cloud of breath as it leaves your body. As you smile at the families walking past you that smile feels true and real.

Solicitor You've just had the last meeting with a client who has had a challenging time with their divorce after many years of marriage. The client is happy with the outcome and the dreaded scenario has been handled well with no blame on either side. They are pleased with the time it has taken and so are you. You can sense the next step that your client is going to be taking as they move into a new future as a single person. There is a visible breathing out and coming together as you share a small gift with them of a cup of tea to celebrate their new status. They lean in to hug you as a thank you for your hard work and you are ready to receive that hug.

Coach You're in an initial meeting with a client who is nervous about sharing the challenges they face. They consistently put themselves down as being stupid or silly. By focusing on them and not their words, you see the strengths in them that they have yet to see and you reflect them back. You feel the chair beneath you as it supports you to support your client. You are aware of the space around you which enables your client to have space too. Your gaze is relaxed and warm. As the meeting progresses, their breathing gets slower, as does their pace of speaking. They leave the meeting having recognised many of their own strengths.

These are just three little pen portraits of a feeling state we all enjoy. The responses in our body are physical – calm breathing, reduced heart rate, increase in happy hormones. They are also psychological – we feel safe and at ease, we can be empathetic and compassionate to those around us, and we feel a sense of joy, awe and wonder with the world.

It is a time when we are fully connected to our internal state, to the world around us and to the living beings we are sharing our space with. I say living beings here, to mean plants, trees and animals as well as us human beings. Many of us reach that connected state through the stroking of a cat or a dog.

Learning how to regulate ourselves when we feel the stress of overwhelm or the feelings of inertia that can lead to disconnection, is essential for people-helping professionals.

The easiest way to regulate ourselves, as I've hinted at above, is to connect with people around us.

And here is the rub: people-helping professionals, although surrounded by people, can sometimes forget to use the free resources available to them. That's all due to the overwhelm and disconnect which can lead to a lack of confidence.

How do we get regulation when we spend so much of our time in the virtual world? My suggestion is to find ways to be more active as your body may well be suffering from some inertia.

- Once an hour stop and stand up, look out of your window, look for beauty in your surroundings or your office space
- Take a break with other people in your household
- Go to a coffee shop, and chat with the barista
- Put an alarm on and go for an afternoon walk to reinvigorate yourself

But how do you regulate when you are surrounded by others all the time? Here you might notice your stress response has been triggered.

- Close your eyes and place your palms over them. Breathe deeply, cupping your eyes gently
- Breathe out for longer than you breathe in, for a few breaths. Then regulate your breathing to six in and six out, or whatever is comfortable for you. This is the coherent breath and it works a treat

- Put both feet on the floor and settle back into your chair. Have the ground and the chair hold you for a moment or two

- Seek out the company of people who have good energy. Smile and have a laugh and a joke

Learning to notice what is going on in our body is essential for us to recognise the effects of too much or too little change. In previous chapters, I have discussed exteroception, interoception and proprioception as ways to notice body sensations. When we have too much change, we need to look to neuroception, the channel of perception that focuses on safety.

If the body is not feeling safe, it will respond by going into hyperarousal or hypoarousal. 'Just right' can be a bit out of reach.

A little technique that I use with my coaching clients: A Somatic ABC.

These are the building blocks that support us to be in ventral vagal. And as with all the tools I am offering you, it is very simple and can be done in less than three minutes.

I will explain how this works over the page.

The Change Flywheel

A ALIGN

B BREATHE

C CENTRE

D DECIDE

E ENGAGE

F FUN

Change

A – ALIGN With a gentle shake, straighten up your body, allowing your spine and pelvis to take more of your weight, shoulders slightly back, giving more space for your lungs.

B – BREATHE With more space your lungs can be properly filled, pushing your diaphragm down, and breathing deeply into your gut.

C – CENTRE 'C' equals centre. In a sitting or standing position, with tiny movements, imagine a string from the top of your head to the ceiling, taking some of the weight of your skull, lengthening the neck and widening your gaze.

If you are with others and you need to speak, then make use of D, E and F.

D – DECIDE Give yourself a moment to make a decision about what has been said or what you might want to say.

E – ENGAGE 'E' equals engage. Only when you are centred and ready, choose to engage, offering eye contact to everyone around you.

F – FUN 'F' equals fun! Work does not have to be serious all the time. Smile or joke; a little fun goes a long way to allowing curiosity and creativity to unfold in your team.

The ABC tool is all about supporting you to be in the state of ventral vagal, a space for connection and creativity.

What difference does change make to how I lead?

For us people-helping professionals, here is the challenge: often we like a steady and stable ship, similar to the cruise liner of old. By keeping things steady, we think we are providing a calm and safe space for people to work. Unfortunately, in our world of rapid change, keeping to the status quo can also cause unnecessary stress and disconnection. In our eagerness to keep people safe, we end up getting ourselves and others in our team stuck.

Supporting yourself to have a better, more energised relationship to change helps everyone know when to say yes and when to say no to changes coming from outside an organisation. Safety is necessary as it is the building block for growth. Remember this chapter is about transformation. Transformation won't happen if we and others are not psychologically safe.

Timothy R. Clarke[64] outlines a practical way that leaders can transform their teams so that members feel included and safe to learn, to contribute and to challenge, ensuring that the organisation deals with change in a resilient way. People-helping professionals would do well to have open discussions with their team about how to make the space psychologically safe. As with all the things I am offering, this doesn't have to be hard. It does require the leader to be emotionally self-managing, however, through working on their resilience, resourcing themselves through rest and regulating themselves.

Lastly, I want to return to the definition of resilience – our ability to adapt, our capacity for change. This definition is so closely linked to energy. With increased capacity, we can be more adaptable. Adaptability is our strength but can also be our weakness. When we are over-stressed or slightly depressed we can be caught off-balance and make changes that are not helpful to ourselves or our team. We may get swayed by the opinions of others or find it hard to say no. It is easier to be adaptable when we are fully rested as we have more energy to give thought to the strategic direction of our work, as well as the tactical day-to-day.

Using the qigong teaching from fellow Somatic coach Gabriela Alvarez Jurgenson,[65] I am going to return to the plant world here to offer you a favourite metaphor for adaptable leadership. Imagine a lush grove of bamboo, reaching up to the sun and rain. It has very deep roots and a slender and flexible trunk. When the wind blows, the flexible stem and deep roots ensure that it is not knocked off balance. Thinking about this metaphor for you as a leader, how could you deepen your roots? Where could you be more flexible, thus showing adaptability?

Energising yourself through the consistent use of *The Change Flywheel* can help you become a leader who can navigate change, switching from the trusty cruise liner to the nifty yacht, as and when necessary. That consistency can support you in dealing with overwhelm and disconnect, giving you the ability to say no and yes when necessary. Consistent practice helps you to be a credible leader in the eyes of your team and clients. All of this goes a long way in empowering you to be confident in your ability to deal with change, to work with the bigger picture, and to effect sustained changes to make our world a better place.

Your pace will be steady and sure – in fact, just right.

CHANGE FLYWHEEL TAKEAWAYS

CHANGE – energise yourself

- Too much, too little or just right. What is the effect of change on your body and mind right now?

- Sleep, think, eat, move. Which of these needs more TLC?

- Which type of rest would benefit from a refresh?

- How can you 'be more bamboo' in your work and home life?

How can using change help me to build an energised me?

Using our power of forethought is an essential way to build more energy. We are fortunate as humans to have this ability to project ourselves into the future and imagine a possibility that has not yet occurred. All energy is neutral; it is our choice to make it positive or negative. We can choose to be more positive.

Activity 1: Writing a letter from your future self

Time needed to write: 30 minutes

Aim: to develop unlimited imagination

This activity comes from Carol Dweck, who does this regularly with her student groups. It's about using your imagination to project a more powerful you: the growth mindset challenge letter.

With a sheet of writing paper or maybe a greeting card (or the space over the page), write yourself a letter from your future self, twenty years from now, to the person you are today.

As you write, be sure to include:

- both the challenges and successes you have had on your journey.
- how you balanced rest and work.
- What good habits you put into your life to mitigate overwhelm, disconnect and a lack of confidence.
- what you would do differently if you were to do those twenty years again.

The Change Flywheel

I have written a letter just like this and I know that if we allow ourselves to communicate deeply with our subconscious mind, we can discover what is holding us back. Identifying these restraints in writing is an energising way to let them go.

To get your mind ready for writing, take time to read and apply the activities in my chapter on creativity.

Activity 2: Ignite energy through play

Time needed: half an hour each day

Aim: to practise getting your brain into an energised state.

In the words of Plato : 'Life must be lived as play.'

Remember the 'F' in my ABC. What stops us from playing? And how can we get more play into our days?

A playful attitude or intention can be applied to any activity. Playful intent can relieve stress, which is the enemy of creativity. It can improve brain function, keeps us connected to others, acts as a stimulus and raises our energy.

So what kind of play could you put into your day?

It might be solo play – choose a short board game or card game, a word puzzle or maybe 100 skips.

It might be playing with others, such as telling jokes, a board game, cards, a game of table tennis or a kickabout with a football.

Or it might be playing with a pet, such as throwing a ball or hide and seek.

Whatever it is, let your inner child come out. When that happens you will become disproportionately curious about your world. Time will slow down as you get into that state of play. After the play session, take your focus back to the area of your life that you want to change in some way. Notice how priming your brain for reflection after play has the effect of expanding your bandwidth.

INTERVIEW WITH ME!

When you read both my life story and my musings on each of the five values of my *Change Flywheel* coaching model, you will learn how I have adapted to change in my world.

Introduction

It seemed only right that I also answer the questions I have asked others in my life and in the interviews included in this book. In reading my responses, you get a little more insight into the areas that are most important to me now as I end this chapter on change.

Thank you to Tracy Starreveld, my copy editor, who turned the tables on me and asked me my five questions.

Five questions about your work and approach to life

Curiosity

In the words of Stephen Hawking: *'Remember to look up at the stars and not down at your feet. Try to make sense of what you see and wonder about what makes the universe exist. Be **curious**. And however difficult life may seem, there is always something you can do and succeed at.'*

How do you keep your curiosity alive in the work that you do today?

As a Leadership Energy Coach, I know that curiosity is essential in my work. I keep that alive by trying to keep judgement out of the room. Judgement or superiority can shut down curiosity, so I keep in mind that while there may be much I do know about a person there is also so much I don't know. When I work with a client or a team, I know their job title, their name, maybe their gender and possibly their sexuality – there will be clues to all of this in the way they show up and what they say. But I also keep in mind the iceberg metaphor: that there is much I can see above the water but the bulk of the iceberg remains below it.

I also tune into how I'm feeling energetically with people: with some, I get a positive feeling, with others not. When someone is projecting a more dulled energy, I am curious as to what might be creating that particular type of feeling. It is a bit like going through a maze, being a detective and looking for clues. Sometimes the magnifying glass comes out, while other times I zoom up away from my client to get a different perspective. Questions are my friends but most of all it is the quality of my presence that supports my clients to get curious about themselves.

In life, I remain curious by using my camera phone as an extension of my eyes. I regularly photograph things that catch my eye, mostly in the natural world. Today, I walked past a tree that I have passed at least 100 times. This afternoon it stopped me in my tracks. The shade of the berries and the way the light caught them was breathtaking. That stopping to savour gives me time to resource myself, taking some of that beauty into me. These pause points help me to tune into living things in my world and to communicate with them. I may not say the words aloud but I am saying to that tree, 'Gosh, you really are very beautiful.'

In my work as a somatic trainer, I now know that I am using a technique called sourcing or loving presence. It comes from Hakomi and the work of Ron Kurtz.[66] As I source from the natural world, I beam back that beauty in my response – in the same way that I do with clients. Sometimes my clients may not recognise the gifts that they have and in receiving them back from me, there is an opportunity to use these gifts to move themselves forward.

> '*Loving presence is a state of being. It is pleasant, very good for one's health, rewarding in and of itself. It's a state in which one is open-hearted and well-intentioned. In its purest form, it is spiritually nourishing and sensitive to subtle energies. It is also the best state to be in when offering someone emotional support.*'
>
> Ron Kurtz and Donna Martin

Courage

It takes courage to be a leader. Thinking about the key leaders in your life, how did the courage they showed in their life support you to be courageous in yours?

I mention the courage of my parents in my journey, but I would like to expand a little on this here, starting with my Dad. Without enough forethought and planning, he did make the jump from one country to another which was a very courageous if a little foolhardy thing to do. Setting up a new business and getting to know others was a real challenge, particularly in the fifties and sixties when there was very obvious racism around. He was courageous in the way he constantly reinvented himself and tried new things, which he carried on into his eighties.

My mum also reinvented herself from a teacher of dressmaking in Sri Lanka to a self-employed dressmaker in the UK. She showed great courage when she divorced my father after 32 years of marriage. My mum was a strict Catholic so this would have been very challenging and courageous of her. She reinvented herself when she started teaching again in her early sixties and grew her community around her. She put on fashion shows with her students and worked for a designer in London.

My mum also travelled at this later stage in her life, going to European countries with a trusted group of friends. Her last international trip was to Sri Lanka at the age of 90 where she climbed aboard a train into Colombo, not put off by the high steps and busy compartments. Nothing was going to stop her from doing what she wanted to do.

Another courageous leader in my life was a nun, Sister Antony, who taught me when I was nine and with whom I have kept in contact. She had and still has a generosity of spirit that I admire in faith leaders who truly connect with their community. She changed her desire to be a fashion designer to being a nun, leaving her family at a young age and moving to England. She managed to keep her creativity alive in her work. She still goes into school a couple of times a week to hear readers. Her constancy to her religious beliefs and wearing of her uniform make her stand out from the crowd, but her warmth and love for her work has been ongoing all her life.

I would also mention group leaders who have stood up against something they saw as clearly wrong and made a change: Nelson Mandela, Steve Biko, Desmond Tutu, Martin Luther King, Rosa Parks and all those who challenged the civil rights inequities and the apartheid system, along with leaders such as the Dalai Lama, who lives his life with joy. I see similar qualities in young leaders today, such as Greta Thunberg, or charities such as Choose Love. These are leaders who fight for justice and love for others. Other sources of inspiration for me are those writers who can change the way we think with a single line or a retelling of stories close to our hearts. True and lasting favourites are women who write with great courage – Maya Angelou and Robyn Hobbs, to name but two.

Creativity

In the words of the late great Sir Ken Robinson: *'I believe this passionately – that we don't grow into creativity; we grow out of it or rather we get educated out of it.'*

What advice would you give schools to help children develop their creative thinking?

Very simple – let children learn with their bodies, to be as practical and active as possible with their learning. We learn about the world through our bodies as babies, rolling over, standing up and walking towards people. Children need to walk towards and be involved in learning and have fun doing this. They need to use hands, creative activity, music, dance, pottery, play – all the arts. All of this has sadly been squeezed out of our curriculum today.

Developing the use of hands, I would definitely teach crafts from age three through to eighteen. Crafting helps regulate stressed and depressed nervous systems. It brings us back into a more connected state and helps us self-soothe. The repetitive movements involved in woodworking, knitting, pottery and sewing provide space to think. The teachers from the sixties and seventies knew this to be true.

I would also recommend more time given to the reading of books and reading for pleasure. I would have a scheduled reading time every day with an adult, as not everyone has parents who can do this. My siblings read to me as a child because my parents did not have the time or energy to do this.

I would also encourage schools to be flexible with their timekeeping; we all know that the circadian clock of teenagers is slightly later, so why not allow them to start at 10 o'clock? Working in line with the students' bodies rather than with traditions would support creativity as they would not be so tired, particularly in the mornings. Let's encourage schools to work with the seasonal rhythms too, getting outside in all seasons. Remember there is no bad weather, just bad clothing.

I would return to a line that I wrote in my chapter on curiosity: 'Often our education system doesn't favour the dreamers, and the doers are the ones who have centre stage. You have to have both – time to think and time to do.'

In that same chapter, I mentioned the Finnish Education system as one that has the basis of play at its core. In my view, the best all-round creative curriculum for children would bring together this Finnish system with the work of Forest Schools and the best of the Steiner school systems that encourage creative endeavour.

Community

For many years, I have had a postcard above my desk outlining '44 ways to build community'. What communities do you lead or have you led in the past, and what helped them grow?

I'm going to share a very personal community that I love and cherish, born out of a traumatic incident when my home was burgled. Although none of us were hurt, we all faced mental anguish from the event.

The natural instinct when something like this happens is to shut down the house and pull up the drawbridge, but we decided to do something different. That was to start a neighbourhood watch scheme for our street. A month after the incident we threw open our doors and invited everyone on our street into our house.

From that point on, our street group evolved on WhatsApp. We now have two threads, a watch group focused on safety and a news group where we share updates and chatty messages about fabulous plumbers, bountiful crops of tomatoes and more.

Eight years on and the groups are still well used. People come and people go. What has helped it grow is clear boundaries, a warm welcome and a joy in connecting.

In creating and nurturing this group, I have fully stepped into the '44 ways to build a community' postcard above my desk.[67]

The second example I am going to give is the communities I helped grow in my work as a teacher and headteacher. Although I am no longer in school full time, I still have a lot of contact with the staff and pupils from those schools. They find me on social media, greet me on the street, and the pupils – many of them now young adults – will readily chat with me. In return, I give them my attention and help their own communities to grow. They also remember all the ways they were resourced as children or teachers and take those positive recollections into their working lives or relationships with others.

Lastly, my coach community is very important to me. It is wide and varied. There are people in this community I trained with in 2015, plus coaches I have met on courses I have done since then to enhance my practice. Some of these coaches were originally clients of mine who went on to train as coaches.

As a trainer, I have connections with hundreds of people who lead communities. I help them grow by supporting them to be better coaches as they in turn support me to be a better coach. Coach mentoring and supervision is an area that I am moving into more and more. As an elder coach and someone entering their sixth decade, I'm looking forward to continuing to support this wonderful collaborative group.

And that leads me to the final way that I help all my communities grow. I take these maxims into my life: 'givers gain' and 'collaboration over competition'. If you give with an open heart without expecting anything in return, you will be repaid in many, many ways. Many people call me a super connector and that's part of my skill as a leadership energy coach. Growing communities is all about connecting others for the greater good of all.

Change

Change is the only constant in our lives or so the saying goes. How do you keep harmony in your life and in your work?

How do I do this? By being curious, by delving deep and learning more about myself and the world around me; by being courageous and finding ways to motivate myself; by being creative and enriching myself through creative endeavour, be that writing, reading or crafting; and by supporting my communities in all the ways I can, which in turns supports me. Those four tenets are of prime importance to me – they provide me with harmony and help energise me.

I also do the daily work of getting the balance right between work and rest. When I talk about work, I don't mean just paid work but all the activities in my day, including service to family and friends. This whole book has been written for people-helping professionals. I am one of these so, in effect, it is for me too. I too can get overwhelmed, so I have to put in the rest.

Rest to work is the yin to the yang of life. I remember to put in rest of all types throughout my week and these vary depending on what is going on in my work. Rest provides me with time to reframe my thoughts. For example, recently I had a very busy Tuesday. Instead of getting irritated by the fact that I had to wash my hair, I used this as a time to rest. The repetitive movements of the washing and drying provided my body with a resting spot. At another point in the day, I had only ten minutes to eat my lunch. I could have gone in with the mindset to rush the food but, instead, I used every minute to eat slowly and savour the food in my mouth. It is a state of mind we can cultivate towards the use of our time. These micro and mini moments are essential to supporting our nervous system to stay in an optimal state.

We cannot save time, we can only use time wisely.' Benjamin Hoff, 'The Tao of Pooh'[68]

Lastly, in the ever-increasing world of online distractions, I keep harmony by connecting with my body, orienting myself to my space, connecting with my breath and sensing into the world around me. I pause, ponder and percolate.

SAM'S TAKEAWAYS

Curiosity: What catches your eye? A look, a smile, a nod or something else? Where could that take you today?

Courage: It takes courage to re-invent. What needs re-inventing in your life right now?

Creativity: *'You have to have time to think and time to do.'* What's the balance like in your life right now? How can you be creative and in doing so create time to think?

Community: *'Givers gain'* and *'collaboration over competition'*. How could either of these two maxims work in your life?

Change: In the yin and yang of life, work is yang and rest is yin. How can you use your time to dial up the rest and reduce the overwhelm?

ENDPIECE

I started this book with the notion that people-helping professionals can find themselves pushing the override button in the workplace. This might be in relation to supporting others or other work commitments. Many times, pressing override results in other areas of their life feeling very stretched. This can and sadly often does lead to overwhelm, disconnect and a lack of confidence.

If you're in a people-helping profession, I hope that *The Change Flywheel* is a tool that you keep returning to, to ensure you remain curious, courageous, creative, supported by your community and therefore embodying change.

While we humans tend to overcomplicate things, the 3 Rs of Resilience, Rest (as a way of resourcing) and Regulation are very simple. Ultimately, they support us to be positively energised in our relationship with ourselves and with others.

Relationships underpin *The Change Flywheel*.

Without relationships, we can find ourselves isolated and overburdened.

3 RS = RELATIONSHIP

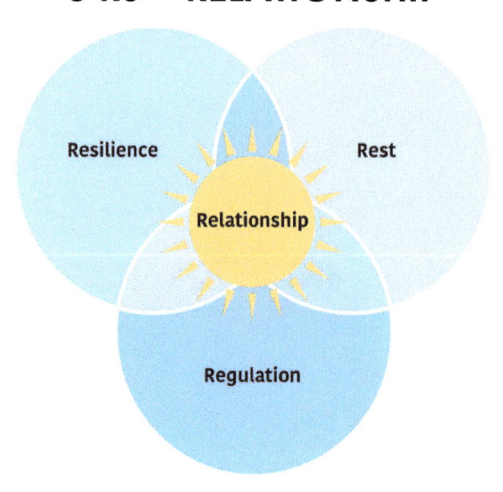

Venn diagram with three overlapping circles labeled Resilience, Rest, and Regulation, with Relationship at the center.

To finish, I am drawn back to the work of Shawn Achor, one of the leading experts on happiness, success and potential. In his book Big Potential,[69] he concludes with a telling reminder about the importance of relationships.

He talks about the Masai warriors of Kenya. When they greet each other they ask 'How are the children?' For everyone, even those without children, the correct answer is 'All the children are well'. He goes on to explain, 'That's because according to their social script, things can't be fully good for one individual unless everyone in the community is thriving.'

In my mind, developing positive relationships with ourselves and others through using *The Change Flywheel* is essential to the success of all people-helping professionals.

It's time to make a switch to this point of view. If we flip the words on their head we get:

> 'How are the leaders?'
> 'All the leaders are well.'

MY JOURNEY

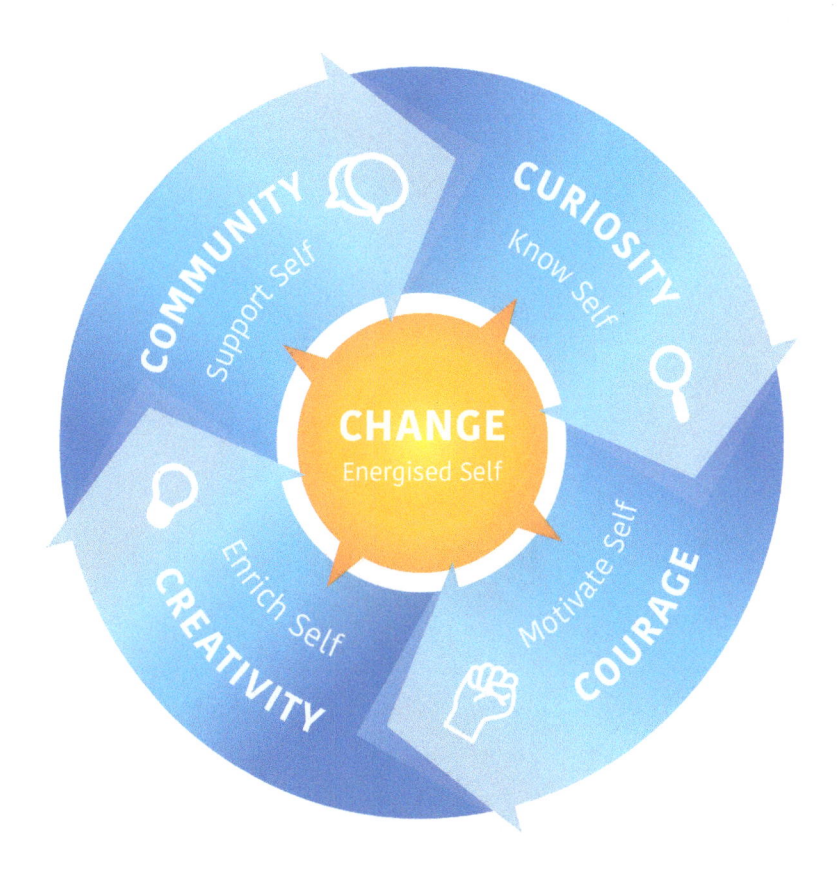

COMMUNITY — Support Self
CURIOSITY — Know Self
COURAGE — Motivate Self
CREATIVITY — Enrich Self

CHANGE — Energised Self

'I seek to live a creative life in thoughts and deeds.'

Sam Jayasuriya

My Journey

If we met on the tube and started to chat, I would tell you that I am a Leadership Energy Coach. It may not have been the job title I was given for various positions I've worked in over the years, but this is what I did.

As a child at primary and secondary school, as a student at college, and later as a teacher and a coach my purpose was to build positive energy in others. In the early days, I sometimes got that wrong. Sometimes I found it hard to manage my own emotions. But through the course of my life and with the help of particular role models who showed up for me, I learned to harness my energy for good.

Early life

I am from a Sri Lankan heritage and was born in Britain, the youngest of five girls. My parents were well-educated and had lived in Sri Lanka for their early adult life. Bigger families were more the norm in that era, particularly for those from a Catholic background such as ours. But the desire for a big family came from my father who had a very 'Asian man' mentality, typical of his generation, and so he yearned for a boy. So for most of my early life, I was known as Sam. I had short hair and was sometimes dressed as a boy, although I very much felt like a girl inside!

My father was a keen photographer and loved taking pictures. On every occasion, you would find him with his camera around his neck. If there was any way that my father showed his love for all of us it would be in his photographs. They captured the seemingly insignificant moments, the ones which I look back on with real fondness – playing in the garden, dressing up or hanging around outside. His photographs of us captured a carefree existence which was juxtaposed with the harsh reality of our everyday life in the 1970s.

My father initially started working in the finance business but turned his hand to many professions throughout his life. I was influenced by his entrepreneurial spirit even though some of his methods cost our family dear when he didn't plan his ventures in a considered way.

My mother worked from the age of eighteen, firstly teaching in a dressmaking school and then opening up her own successful school in Colombo. Dressmaking requires a keen attention to detail and my mother was organised and systematic in her work.

My family's decision to leave Sri Lanka was taken by my father who found small island life to be difficult at times; he wanted a more cosmopolitan lifestyle. My father arrived first in the UK, a year before my mother. She followed after packing up her school in Colombo, arriving with two small babies in the late fifties for a new life. My mother soon realised that to keep food on the table she would need to work as a dressmaker. Rather than taking on piecework, like many other immigrant families of the time, she set herself up as a private dressmaker and slowly but surely grew her client base.

Life was tough when I was born but my parents both worked hard and very long hours.

My mother would work all day whilst we were at school, only stopping to give us a snack when we got home and then working again until it was time to prepare dinner. After this, she would sew late into the night. As a teen, I remember her working until nine or ten at night, or even later. My father was always at work, leaving early in the morning and getting home late at night. There were many times I remember him arriving home after we had eaten and having dinner on his own.

Due to their long working hours during my early years, it was my eldest sister, who is nine years older than me, who looked after me a lot. Until she left home at eighteen, she behaved like a surrogate mother, keeping an eye on all of us as we played out and about. I have many positive memories of those early years, but these were mirrored by a scary relationship with my father. He had an increasingly challenging battle with alcohol and gambling, and his frustration and anger were taken out on all of us. The debts made our family life very precarious: we often ran out of money and the house was mortgaged and remortgaged to pay off the debts owed by his various businesses.

As I grew up, I was very conscious of the difficulties placed on the family by the decisions of both my parents. My father's strengths were being able to connect with others, be creative in his ideas and courageous in moving into new and growing fields. These were overshadowed by his negative coping strategies. My mother's strengths were constancy and competence which kept us from being homeless but, from my perspective, her work also took away her joy.

It is important for me to outline these early years as they played a key part in how I went on to live my life. The financial hardships we experienced back then have shaped my working life. As soon as I was able to, I got a part-time job in a shop at the age of sixteen. Having my own money was very important to me. Making decisions about how I spent that was equally important. I now know from my work that the need for financial well-being because of family trauma is a reason why some people-helping professionals can get stuck in a job.

Some of the key values that I hold in my mind every day were also evident in those early years. The courage of both my parents to move to another country and make a new life; the creativity I saw daily in the work of my mother – in her designs, her use of fabrics and meticulously finished articles of clothing, and in my father – in his imaginings for his business, his photography and his eye for innovation. Community was also key, with the family unit of sisters and parents being very tight. We were surrounded by loving neighbours and belonged to a thriving church community. In these relationships outside the home, I found supportive parent figures who helped me manage the negative emotions I felt towards my father.

As the youngest child, it was hard for me to be a leader at home. There was a strict pecking order in my house. My two eldest sisters seemed slightly out of reach; they were teens when I was in primary school. As the youngest, I had to follow the lead of the next two eldest.

So I looked for leadership roles outside of the family: being a prefect in school, a house captain, a part of the choir, one of the young church leaders, and part of the youth group committee. You name it, I wanted to be on it. The desire to lead was very strong in me and that was initially born out of a need to be noticed and recognised for my own strengths and merits, not just because it was *my turn*.

As with most children, I dreamt of a variety of jobs I wanted to do as an adult, including an artist living in Paris in an old attic and an author of children's stories. As a teen, a keen

My Journey

interest in equality, anti-racism and politics led to a desire to be an activist and set the world to rights.

I chose teaching as a way for me to be a leader and have a steady income, which was how I saw I could make my way in the world.

Early career

After graduating I started my first teaching job at a school in Paddington, a safe haven for the bed-and-breakfast children it served who lived in run-down, cockroach-infested hotels in the area. There was a 200% turnover each year. I was lucky if I had more than five children staying in my class from September through to July. The school was small and each class was a mixed-age group. I worked there for four years.

This school was the place where I learned to build on the resilience that I had cultivated in my childhood. I knew what many of these children were going through. Although I had not been homeless, I had been in a place where food and opportunities were scarce. So I made it my purpose to help open their eyes to the wonders of the world around them.

This was, for me, the best start to a long career in education. Just at the start of the National Curriculum, the testing regime now found in schools was very distant. The headteacher of the time, June Bowie, was in her final two years of headship. Her first thoughts were to the children and how she could ensure they were nurtured in the school. It went without saying that she expected every child to make progress for however long they were there. Following her lead, I learned to build very good relationships quickly with both the children and the parents.

The school was unusual as everyone used first names when talking to each other. The children called me Samantha, or Miss if they wished. It was the same for all members of staff including the headteacher whom they called June. Many people I talked to out of school were shocked that children were allowed to talk to the staff in this way. They assumed that the children would take advantage of this lack of deference and behave badly. I know that this was not true. Respect does not come to people through titles but by the way that they treat others. The children abided by the rules of the school because they knew them to be fair and reasonable. There were no harsh punishments; they were not kept in detention when they erred but talked to in a reasonable manner.

Developing my core values

I learnt from this first school that I needed to show more consistency in the routines I had in place and pack any creative teaching around that structure. The children needed constant figures in their lives who were there to soothe the trauma of temporary accommodation. In that first school, the benefits of teaching assistants were already known as each class had a full-time assistant to support the children. More adults meant more one-to-one time for each child.

The curriculum was very creative with an absolute adherence to the arts, which had as much time in the curriculum as literacy and maths. It was the norm that we had PE and games lessons every week, plus music taken with a trained music teacher and pottery with an art teacher. I knew that their learning needed to be practical and fun. I wanted my class to run excitedly into school each day and then run home again, keen to tell their parents what they had been up to.

This was a school that focused on learning for teachers as well as for students. All the staff were expected to share their personal learning with each other. Teachers here loved to read, write and create. That flourishing community meant that we also put in time for ourselves outside work. The school was locked each day at six o'clock and everyone went home to other things. We undertook art classes together, and learnt to bind books and in doing so we kept ourselves balanced.

At the end of my second year of teaching, we all started to plan June's retirement as she turned sixty. A huge party was planned but then the unthinkable happened: she had a stroke a few weeks before the end of term and died.

Dealing with death is hard in your own family, but when you have to grieve with a whole school it is incredibly painful. But once again, this community of people showed the world how to grieve in a way that allowed all of our emotions to be shared. Every member of staff and many parents attended the funeral. June was much loved but she had one flaw: she did not rest or recuperate but just gave her life to the school. She had planned so much for her retirement but was not able to realise her dreams. I learnt not to put off until tomorrow the things I could do today. I learnt to put in some boundaries and not just live for work. I learnt that to be successful meant having a whole life. June's premature death taught me that.

June's leadership profile sat very much in the style of a 'servant leader'. She was absolutely committed to her team, which was first and foremost the children and then the staff and wider church community. Her mantra was 'children first' and she was a champion for them right up to her death. Her mission in life was clear – to address the inequalities she saw in the world regarding education.

June's successor was Lucy (you will have read her interview on page 149) who shared many of her traits. Lucy was also fully committed to the children – another leader who put the children first. She had an uncanny knack for being able to see the world through the eyes of a child, and her inspirational work on early childhood writing guided me in my work.

If a person could personify zest, then Lucy did just that – in the way she dressed in bright clothes, very atypical of headteachers of that time; in the way she moved her body and the way she spoke. Fundamentally, she modelled for me exactly what teaching was all about. It was about the children and learning had to be fun; when we are having fun, we are more likely to push ourselves out of our comfort zones and take a few risks. Risk-taking and failing with fun equals good learning in my book.

Lucy was, like June, incredibly humble. When complimented, she would brush it off. She was inspired by conversation. Staff would meet in her office after school to chat about children, plans and events. With her feet on the desk in her turquoise leggings, she had an easy air which drew us all in.

In doing so, she created a team who were excited about creativity and looked to make each day an inspirational day for the children.

My Journey

We were encouraged to think out of the box and Lucy did just that. We had impromptu events which showed the children the possibility of doing so much more. One morning, she arranged for a friend to abseil down the side of the building into the internal courtyard. Now that might sound a little dangerous, but many of the children had no experience of sports other than running in the park and what they did at school. That event opened their eyes to learning to challenge themselves and having the courage to overcome their fears.

This excitement created by the many visitors we had at the school was taken to a whole new level in my last year there, when we embarked on six months of working with two artists-in-residence, Richard Layzell and Jerome Ming, both of whom I have interviewed earlier in the book.

Working with creatives in school

Starting in September, the House of Nations was born.

The plan was to investigate how communities around the world used found material to create their own homes. In doing so, we were going to create a House for all Nations out of rubbish in the local area.

All artists have different timescales. I know this as I live with two artists, my husband and my son. It is hard to put boundaries on creativity and I found that out when we were halfway through the project. We sent out messages that we needed rubbish to be collected to help build our structure: a house, big enough to stand in and accommodate the class of thirty children. Now that's a lot of rubbish. Luckily, we had an underground playground where we kept the donated items.

The children turned the rubbish into screens which were pieced together to make the walls of the house and the roof. This was exciting as they were allowed to use tools which were not available to children at that time. There was a lot of risk-taking and creativity in this part of the project.

Lastly, we used fabric and paper to decorate the interior. Colour was key here, and making the structure comforting and beautiful was essential to making it a home.

The joy on the children's faces when we finally visited their artwork house in Southwark Art Gallery will stay with me forever. Out of nothing they created something usable and beautiful.

The 5 Cs start to form

Curiosity was key. As teachers, we helped open the eyes of the pupils through a fully creative and immersive curriculum.

Courage – we were all actively encouraged to step out of our comfort zones, to do things that were a bit different while encouraging the children to do the same.

Creativity was present from the moment you walked through the arched door into a world where we had teaching in pottery, music, book-binding and more. We taught the children that with perseverance and persistence, they could create and make.

Community – this school was a vibrant community that encouraged everyone to show up as themselves. We valued and celebrated the cultural differences of the children.

Change was inevitable. It was the time of the introduction of the national curriculum and slowly, over time, we had to adapt to the new constraints that were put on us. However, we still managed to move that wheel on our terms, in ways that worked for our children.

Self-belief challenges

However, it was here in my first teaching position that I realised that my own need for recognition was still proving difficult. I found it hard to share recognition with others. I still wanted to do things quicker than others. It was hard letting go of the need to be in control and that struggle had me erupting with anger over very silly things.

Lucy could see that I needed support and so arranged for me to have some sessions with Claire Chappell, a wise school advisor whose work as a psychotherapist helped me so much in those early days. She was someone I could open up to about my family's past and my challenging relationship with my father. These were things that I did not share with anyone outside my family. As a result of the trauma I'd experienced, I kept them to myself.

The opportunity to talk openly was a tremendous support for me, and in doing so I was able to disconnect from some of my father's negative behaviour. I was my own person, not a shadow of him. I could be kind, helpful and supportive to others. I did think about the needs of my team and cared about them. I did have my own opinions which I could voice without needing to be right all the time. This was a journey which started here and which continues to this day.

Recently, I reconnected with Lucy and discovered that Claire Chappell had sadly passed away. I wish I had had the opportunity to thank her for the time she spent with me, supporting me in helping me manage my emotions. Claire was my first coach.

War trauma

In my final year of teaching at the school in 1990, the Iraq–Kuwait war broke out. We immediately had political refugees starting in the school, families who had been on holiday in the UK and now could not return to their country. It was heartbreaking for them to hear of the war back home. The only thing we could do was to make the children feel safe by welcoming them into the fold. They were quickly welcomed in and mostly stayed on until well after the war had finished.

What we gave them that year was hope, peace and harmony in their lives:

Hope – that there is acceptance in the world; that learning can continue; and that they would be safe.

Peace – to live amongst different cultures and still be themselves; to share their traditions and beliefs, and not be judged.

Harmony – that whatever was happening at home was not happening here; that here, the learning continued; that we would show empathy for their situation but not smother them with overconcern.

Moving on and stepping up

But time and tide wait for no man or woman, and my desire to grow led to my first move to a new school. I had always set my sights on being a headteacher by the time I was forty and also on having children by the same age. I moved to another school in Westminster and courage was a value which played a great part in my work there.

I was bowled over by the charismatic head who appointed me, Ricci Achillini. He was dynamic and a definite go-getter. He had an easy relationship with the children, similar to Lucy and June. The school was filled with keen aspirational leaders as well as some staff who were good teachers but who found change a challenge.

It was in this school that I learnt the meaning of the word courage as I stepped quickly into an acting deputy head role in my sixth year of teaching, supporting the school through a transition. I loved working in this way, knowing that I was moving forward with my plans to be a head. I had to learn to adapt my style to meet the needs of two very different headteachers, one of whom wanted to keep the school ticking over by sorting out procedures and processes. Their style was what the school needed at that moment. The second was new to headship but ready to lead and had very strong views on how they wanted to do that.

After learning so much from this team and the new deputy head, I moved on to working in another school in a completely different area of London. Up to now, I had worked primarily in inner London, with children who mostly came from socially deprived backgrounds and in temporary housing. I wanted a new challenge and applied and started working as a deputy head in another school, this time in the leafy suburbs.

Although I lived in the suburbs, the move away from working in inner London was a big step for me. I loved working in the centre of London and enjoyed the hustle and bustle of the streets. I had taught in a creative way using the resources on our doorstep to enrich the lives of the children. I had no hesitation in walking children across Hyde Park to visit museums and galleries.

A move to the suburbs felt a little like I was cutting myself off from the riches of the city. But I didn't need to worry as this particular environment taught me much more.

The immediate feel of the school was that it was steeped in tradition, and I am not saying that in a negative way. I too mark my life with traditional events which remind me of my part in the world. But a few of the traditions in this school needed a bit of a refresh. We did things just because they had always been done that way, not to enrich the lives of the children.

Working with John Hewer was a gift for me. I learnt so much from him. He helped me see that as a head you had to balance dynamism with steadiness. Leading a school can sometimes feel like you are steering a huge cruise liner. My gift to that school was to allow it to change its shape from time to time from that liner to a nifty yacht.

We retained many of the traditions which kept the community close but broadened the view out of the school to invite in more performers and professional artists to work with the children.

And the children thrived on this: in the years that I worked there, they had numerous opportunities to work out of the school. Those opportunities opened their eyes to a world of work that they could not imagine. I still meet many of these pupils in my local community and am always heartened by their very positive memories of their primary school life.

Many creative projects stick in my mind. One, in particular, I hold dear. A newly qualified teacher had built a huge Viking boat in her classroom as part of a history project related to the Vikings to teach the children about traditional life and rituals. One day, she said to me, despairing: 'I don't know what to do with it.' My reply was that it needed to be burnt, just as they did in Viking days. That led to her organising with her year group partners a ceremonial burning of the boat. Every child got dressed up in Viking clothes, along with the staff who led the ceremony in the playground that day.

As the ash floated over the playground and we all started to cough, I knew that the staff had created memories that would not be forgotten. The learning had been embedded deep. These children had experienced something that they could pass on to their own children in years to come. That new teacher is now a school head and I am pretty confident she will be leading her school in creative ways and enriching their learning.

It takes courage to change and let go

It was here that I took the courageous step of ending my first marriage and the school I worked in supported me through that challenging time. I had married my best friend who was wonderful as a friend but our core values were not aligned and our marriage was faltering. I was incredibly fortunate in my early thirties to meet my second husband Carl who

I immediately knew was the person for me. Within six months of meeting, we were engaged and then we married within a year. On our first wedding anniversary, we brought home our oldest son and in two years I went on to have my youngest son.

Headship and motherhood – a match made in heaven!

During this time, I carried on working full-time as a headteacher, balancing my home and work life. I was fully supported by my partner, family and an amazing childminder (thank you Debbie Jones). I put strict boundaries into my working day, which was very different to some of my contemporaries. As soon as I had dropped off my boys at 7.45 am I put my headteacher hat on, and when I picked them up at 6 pm I switched back to being a mum. These early days of motherhood were challenging and there were times I found it hard to keep my own creative thoughts going.

Being a mother was a gift not just to my partner and me but also to my career. On maternity leave, the amazing deputies I worked with would step up to the position of acting head. When I returned they would embark on their own journeys and become headteachers themselves. Over the years, I have worked with or recruited at least six teachers who went on to be heads in their own right. I am so proud to have been part of their leadership journey. After all, it is our job as leaders to grow new leaders.

Coach development

Coaching has been part of my life since those early days of being a deputy and a headteacher. I was fortunate to be part of coach training in the early 2000s at the Institute of Education and was a very early adopter of working with a coach in my first headship. Working with a coach helped me to get perspective on my role as a head and as Sam, the person. Working through genuinely good leadership programmes with my local authority, I learnt more and more about leadership and what it meant to be a good leader. I recognised that there was an imbalance in my coaching style as a leader, including a more coercive 'this is what needs to be done' approach which didn't allow for different methods to be employed.

After thirteen years, the time came for me to move on from this wonderful school. My gift to them was a box of seeds and a rose so that they could continue to give everyone who entered the school a warm welcome. To this day, that same rose continues to grace the arbour by the gate and I know that the school maintains its presence as a creative school in my local community.

Two heads are better than one

As my boys grew older, I knew I wanted to spend time with them, but as a headteacher that possibility seemed so out of reach. I enjoyed leadership and also enjoyed being a parent and didn't want to give up one for the other. The opportunity to jointly lead a school came up. I applied and was fortunate to get a co-headship which lasted for five years. My partner head, Jude Stone, had different strengths to me and that was what made the relationship work.

The school was in a precarious position with falling rolls given its geographical position where it was surrounded by schools with 'good' and 'outstanding' external gradings. Constant competition meant that on occasion we felt forced to put into practice changes that didn't suit our community.

We were intent on providing high-quality teaching and good learning, but many of the challenges faced by the families made it very hard for their children to access what the school down the road took for granted.

One of my main successes with my co-head at this school was to re-establish good connections with a large section of the parent body. We did what all good leaders should do. We stood at the gate and engaged with the parents. We were available every day to hear their concerns and join in with their celebrations. I know that this is the norm for many schools nowadays and particularly during the Covid 19 pandemic and period of lockdowns. But back then it wasn't so well known or practised.

Reflecting back, my life as a co-head was incredibly fulfilling. Time away from school gave me the chance to reconnect with my creative endeavours. This was something which had been missing; creativity had been squeezed out by motherhood, headship and being a supportive partner.

Putting creativity back into my life in the form of knitting was very valuable to me. It allowed me space to breathe away from work and to turn my mind to the beauty of seeing something appearing in between my fingers. It taught me perseverance and persistence and helped me slow down. After about three years, I began to yearn for full-time work again and returned to full-time headship.

Where the oak trees stand

The last school I worked in as a head provided me with time to pause and breathe.

The space outside was quite breathtaking; the school had been in existence since the 1950s but the trees were much older. Huge oaks towered around the edge of the field and I could see how the place would have looked many years ago – with those trees marking out the territory of the farmers' land. I used these old oaks as inspiration for my first published poem. (see appendix)

The majesty of these old trees created a safe haven for the children and staff in that school, and this was one of the things I loved about working there. The school served a mostly socially deprived area in the local authority, but that was beginning to change. There were also many new communities moving into the area. There were changes needed within the school's systems too and some of the old familiar practices had to go.

In a similar way to the work I had done in previous schools, I worked together with the staff to create new traditions for the school while also letting go of some of the older ones which they had outgrown. We looked in detail at what made the school tick, what we valued and held dear as an organisation. I invited the staff to look with a critical eye at how we were using the space and to think creatively about new ways to work.

The staff, parents and children stepped up to the challenge. Once they knew that their point of view mattered they were more than happy to share. Staff members who may never have spoken up before now developed, growing into senior leaders in the school. For the first time, the pupils had a voice and were heard; and when that happened, I used their energy to propel us forward.

It was in this school that I fully stepped into my coaching abilities. I used a coaching style of leadership and with my senior team, we developed our coaching culture. I informally coached several members of staff to help them see their potential and step out of their comfort zones. In this, I was encouraging them to take on leadership positions or new roles in the school and to try out new ideas.

We embarked on building a new 'nurture space' right in the heart of the school and an outdoor library that the children could access during breaks and lunchtimes. Who says you can't have books in the playground?

It was here that my confidence as a leader flourished. In my tours with prospective parents, I made it very clear that at the heart of the school was a commitment to the emotional, mental and physical well-being of not just the children but the staff too. It was here that I modelled what self-care looked like and how easy it could be using the inspiring environment we had.

This staff group were always very close, but by extending some of the practices a little, the whole community could get involved. Staff well-being lunches became the norm; we gardened together outside; we had shout-out walls to recognise small acts of kindness; and the expectation was set that we all had agency over ourselves and the way we worked.

I told the parents that they would know if their children were happy at school by the way they ran into school in the morning and ran home in the afternoon to tell them all they had done. And this was just as I had wanted it at my previous schools too, so many years before.

That's what we created over time. The doors were flung open and we welcomed in a community that wanted to grow the school. The PTA was reformed, the governing body re-modelled, and I managed to harness the energy of the group to create a wonderful school. It was here that I decided to use my strengths as a connector and chose to work with the talented writer, Jonny Zucker, who became our author-in-residence until he died prematurely in 2017.

It was at this time that I started my formal coach training as I knew that moving into another full-time headship was not for me. I knew that my time building school communities was done and that my work bringing out the potential in others went beyond the school gates.

After dipping my toe in the coaching world, I was ready to take the leap. I did this with a steady resolve, leaving my full-time position to go into another co-headship with the warm and nurturing Donna Humbles.

Before I left, I recognised that it was in this school that my own coaching model had been formulated, weaving together all the threads in a journey that had started back in September 1987 as a new teacher ready to face my first class.

This was the point in my journey that *The Change Flywheel* was born.

I knew that to be truly authentic leaders, we needed to be **curious**, **courageous** and **creative**, and use our **community** to bring about positive **change** – for ourselves and others.

Having worked in education for thirty years, under sixteen education ministers, surviving seven Ofsted inspections, and having worked with hundreds of children, staff members, parents and governors – I knew I had the experience and the tools to carve out a new career path as a Leadership Energy Coach working with people-helping professionals.

Now I work as a coach for individuals and teams. I am a coach trainer supporting coaches to learn to work with the authority of the physical body. I support teams to develop a coaching culture in their organisations. I am a coach-mentor, speaker and author. I've kept that love of learning and joy in working with others consistently throughout my whole life. My *Change Flywheel* has supported me professionally and personally to be curious, to keep motivated, to enrich myself, to use and support my community and to harness that energy for good.

APPENDIX

A line of Oaks

How do you track time?
Is it by the seasons?
The light as it lengthens and shortens across the year?
Is it by the moon as it waxes and wanes?
Or by the stars, as they make their celestial way across the sky?
Do you track time by the sowing of seeds, the lambing of sheep or the harvest of grain?
I track time by my observations of the oaks.
That stand in a line on the edge of the field by the village hall.
A line of age
Planted by intent
To map out belonging.
A line which has lasted two hundred years or more.
A line of memories of countless children that have swung and climbed the branches, who grew and outgrew their socks, shoes and homes.
A line of time shown by the thickening girth
And countless rings which hide beneath the rustling branches.
A line of six whose presence gives protection from summer sun and driving rain when caught out on a walk.
And shelter to those who need time to think, time to pray, and time to whisper sweet nothings in each other's ears.
I track time by their leaves that grow, flourish and fall.
A line of age.
A line of memories.
A line of time.
A line of oaks.

Samantha Jayasuriya

ACKNOWLEDGEMENTS

This book has come together with the support and encouragement of many people, some living and some no longer here.

I could say this is everyone I have been in contact with throughout my whole life. However, there have been some key players whom I'd like to thank here.

Writing supports and guides

Tracy Starreveld, for her invaluable writing support and whose editorial input and copy editing skills have been applied so gently and firmly. I hope my love of double spacing that littered my writing hasn't overwhelmed you.

Carl, my wonderful and supportive husband, who has put up with my very early morning chats when inspiration has tended to strike me. That darkest hour before dawn is for me the most enlightening of times. He has also been relentless in spotting those weasel words that love to creep into my writing – so, really and very. I love you lots, dear words, but be gone back to the wild woods from whence you came.

The Whalebone Writers Group who have helped me form a regular habit around writing.

Illustrators and designers

Carl, again, for his wonderful original interpretation of my *Change Flywheel*.

Jennifer Yen of Westeast Design who entered my brain and enhanced the idea.

Suzie Hacker, an illustrator and visual designer, whose creative endeavour helped me set free my ABC, yin-yang motif and the 7 types of rest.

My publisher, Sarah Houldcroft and her team at Goldcrest Books, for enhancing and sharing my work so beautifully.

Coaches and mentors

My dearest eldest sister Melinda, who has featured in the book and been so constant despite the many challenges she has faced in recent years.

To all the leaders in my life who agreed to be interviewed – Viv Grant, Dara Caryotis, Richard Layzell, Jerome Ming, Lucy Scott-Ashe, Heather Waring and Ingrid Fetell Lee.

My wonderful coach friends who inspire me so much. Carol Pearson and Rebecca Walker – your energy is truly restorative.

Thank you to the AoEC community, in particular Karen Smart, and of course Jenny Campbell from the Resilience Dynamic, whose words you will have read in the foreword.

To all those who have coached me over the past few years,

particularly Reshma Jobanputra who helped me get this book off the starting blocks and Sarah James Wright who championed me as I approached the end.

To Yvette Elcock, a wonderful supervisor who kept me digging deep.

Thank you to The Somatic School community and in particular Sam Taylor and Nathan Blair, for their teaching around the authority of the body.

To the leaders whom I have mentioned in my book and all those I haven't. Please don't think just because your name isn't here that you are not important because you are. Your relationship with me helped me to develop and lead with confidence, reduce the overwhelm and connect to myself.

To the late great author Jonny Zucker, who inspired me to write. Your zany love of words and magic tricks captivated me as much as the children I worked with.

Lastly, the adults I work with now and the children I worked with in the past. You have always been my inspiration and hope for a better and more energised future.

ABOUT THE AUTHOR

Sam Jayasuriya is a Professional Certified Coach with the ICF, a global leadership energy coach, coach trainer, coach mentor and teacher. Sam's unique coaching style was honed over decades with 20 years as a headteacher across three schools.

Sam seeks to be creative in thoughts and deeds. She loves to read, write and create.

sam@sunskycoaching.co.uk
www.sunskycoaching.co.uk
www.linkedin.com/in/samantha-jayasuriya/

REFERENCES

Following are references linked to each chapter and interview

Introduction

Curiosity

1. Porges is the author of 'The Polyvagal Theory: Neurophysiological Foundations of Emotions, Attachment, Communication, and Self-regulation' (Norton, 2011).
2. https://www.mariolivio.com/mario-livios-books.html
3. https://worldpopulationreview.com/country-rankings/pisa-scores-by-country
4. https://www.theguardian.com/education/2016/sep/20/grammar-schools-play-europe-top-education-system-finland-daycare
5. https://www.theguardian.com/science/2021/aug/15/the-hidden-sense-shaping-your-wellbeing-interoception
6. https://www.danielgoleman.info/
7. https://www.youtube.com/watch?v=sKmKKCdnJ4U
8. https://youtu.be/N5oRhCOyeAg
9. https://www.youtube.com/watch?v=_56GhHgGU2U

Dara Caryotis

10. Designed and developed by Marvin Oka and Grant Soosalu, mBIT enables us to establish communication with our multiple brains, ensure each brain is operating from its highest expression and then apply that highest expression

for greater wisdom in decision-making and action-taking. Informed by the latest Neuroscience findings, along with techniques and concepts from Positive Psychology, Cognitive Linguistics, Behavioural Modeling and NLP, you will learn leading edge models for aligning your head, heart and gut brains and producing incredible results in your own and other's performance.

11 https://en.wikipedia.org/wiki/Gregory_Bateson

12 Compassionate Curiosity – the ability to dig for more information without judgement while simultaneously identifying with how that person is feeling/thinking

13 https://laineykeogh.com/

14 https://www.ted.com/talks/sir_ken_robinson_do_schools_kill_creativity?language=en

Courage

15   http://www.lionswhiskers.com/

16 https://www.ted.com/talks/carol_dweck_the_power_of_believing_that_you_can_improve?language=en

17 https://www.paulineroseclance.com/pdf/ip_high_achieving_women.pdf

18 https://lifeandleadershippodcast.libsyn.com/the-imposter-syndrome-with-dr-valerie-young?utm_sq=g5t81x5s3s

19 https://thework.com/2017/10/four-liberating-questions/

20 https://hbr.org/2021/02/stop-telling-women-they-have-imposter-syndrome

21 https://www.youtube.com/watch?v=zMRcWj_GKxY

22   https://www.mbraining.com/

23 https://www.cam.ac.uk/stories/microbiome-kingdom-of-the-gut

24 https://www.amazon.co.uk/Focusing-Direct-Knowledge-Feelings-Intuition/dp/184413220X

25 https://seths.blog/2016/04/the-distance/

26 https://markmanson.net/limiting-beliefs

27 https://www.nhs.uk/live-well/exercise/running-and-aerobic-exercises/get-running-with-couch-to-5k/

Viv Grant

28 Warner type questions tackle these areas -
- Motivation to Work with children and young people
- Emotional awareness and ability to self-reflect
- Working within professional boundaries and self-awareness
- Ability to safeguard and promote the welfare of children and young people.

Creativity

29 R.J. Sternberg, T.I. Lubart, 'Investing in creativity', American Psychologist, 51 (7) (1996), pp. 677-688

30 'The Tao of Pooh' - Benjamin Hoff, ISBN-10: 1405293780

31 https://www.theguardian.com/lifeandstyle/2023/jun/18/self-and-wellbeing-polycrisis-time-anxiety

32 'The Artist's Way' – Julia Cameron, ISBN: 9780143129257

33 https://news.usm.my/index.php/english-news/4854-5-main-characteristics-of-creative-people-see-if-you-have-any-of-those

34 Divergent - the process of separating from the status quo.

Ingrid Fetell Lee

35 https://www.ted.com/talks/ingrid_fetell_lee_where_joy_hides_and_how_to_find_it?language=en

Lucy Scott-Ashe

36 https://www.horniman.ac.uk/

37 https://dera.ioe.ac.uk/id/eprint/4739/1/Excellence_in_Cities_and_Education_Action_Zones_management_and_impact_(PDF_format)[1].pdf

38 https://educationhub.blog.gov.uk/2022/05/05/everything-you-need-to-know-about-sats/

Community

39 'A General Theory of Love' – Thomas Lewis, M.D., Fari Amini, M.D., Richard Lannon, M.D.

40 Pg 114 'A General Theory of Love' – Thomas Lewis, M.D., Fari Amini, M.D., Richard Lannon, M.D.

41 Pg 157 'A General Theory of Love'.

42 **Ravelry** is a community site, an organisational tool, and a yarn & pattern database for knitters and crocheters.

43 https://pubmed.ncbi.nlm.nih.gov/25910392/

44 https://www.campaigntoendloneliness.org/health-impact/

45 https://www.campaigntoendloneliness.org/facts-and-statistics/

46 https://www.actionforchildren.org.uk/

47 https://www.rhythmofregulation.com/

48 Neuroception refers to the neural circuits that allow our bodies to register whether an environment is safe or dangerous.

49 https://georgekohlrieser.com/publications/unleash-potential-as-a-secure-base-leader/

50 https://www.forbes.com/sites/forbescoachescouncil/2019/09/13/the-benefits-of-cultural-diversity-in-the-workplace/

References

51   https://www.mindtools.com/aqnm32z/how-to-thrive-in-a-multi-generational-workplace

52   https://www.joyuncensored.co.uk/about

53   https://hagitude.org/

Change

54   https://en.wikipedia.org/wiki/Heraclitus

55   https://en.wikipedia.org/wiki/Seneca_the_Younger

56   https://www.mheducation.co.uk/resilience-a-practical-guide-for-coaches-9780335263745-emea-group

57   https://mybook.to/Resilience-Dynamic

58   https://www.amazon.co.uk/Pillar-Plan-Relax-Longer-Healthier/dp/0241303559/ref=tmm_pap_swatch_0?_encoding=UTF8&qid=1701603932&sr=1-1

59   https://www.annearcherassociates.com/

60   https://www.science.org/content/article/wood-wide-web-underground-network-microbes-connects-trees-mapped-first-time

61   https://thedobook.co

62   https://en.wikipedia.org/wiki/Sisyphus

63   https://youtu.be/ZGNN4EPJzGk

64   https://www.amazon.co.uk/4-Stages-Psychological-Safety/dp/1523087684

65   https://www.linkedin.com/in/jurgenson/

Sam Jayasuriya

66   https://mindfulselfdiscovery.com/the-practice-of-loving-presence/

67 https://www.syracuseculturalworkers.com/products/postcard-how-to-build-community

68 https://www.amazon.co.uk/Tao-Pooh-Wisdom/dp/1405204265

End piece

69 https://www.shawnachor.com/books/big-potential/

Contact details for some of the interviewees

Dara Caryotis
https://www.linkedin.com/in/dara-caryotis-822583/overlay/contact-info/

Viv Grant
https://www.integritycoaching.co.uk/

Jerome Ming
https://jeromeming.com/

Ingrid Fetell Lee
https://aestheticsofjoy.com/

Richard Layzell
https://thenamingorg.wordpress.com/

Heather Waring
http://womenwalkingwomentalking.com/about/

Milton Keynes UK
Ingram Content Group UK Ltd.
UKHW052122250224
438371UK00001B/4